Patriot Dreams

The Murder of
Colonel Rich Higgins, USMC

Robin Higgins

Edited by Richard N. Côté

Foreword by General A. M. Gray, Jr.
29th Commmandant of the U.S. Marine Corps

Hellgate Press
Central Point, Oregon

HELLGATE PRESS
An imprint of PSI Research
P.O. Box 3727
Central Point, Oregon 97502
541/245-6502
info@psi-research.com

Cover design by James Young

Higgins, Robin, 1950-
  Patriot dreams: the murder of Colonel Rich Higgins, USMC / Robin Higgins; edited by Richard N. Côté; foreword by A.M. Gray, Jr.
    p.cm.
  ISBN 1-55571-527-3 (cloth)
    1. Lebanon—History—Civil War, 1975-1990. 2. Higgins, Rich, 1945---Assassination. 3. Hostages—Lebanon. 4 Hostages—United States. 5 United States Marine Corps—Officers—Biography. I. Côté, Richard N. II. Title

DS87.52.H54 2000
956.9204'4—dc21
                                              00-040999

Dedication

I thank my grandmothers for the strong, proud, smart woman genes.

I thank my parents for bringing up four kids who all came of age in the 60s.

I thank my mentors, none of whom I dare mention by name fearing I'd leave someone out.

I thank the generals and the privates for looking out for me.

And,

To Richard

Semper Fidelis

Always Faithful

Acknowledgement

It is not my intent to malign or belittle, sadden or madden, or to open old wounds unnecessarily. I merely want to tell the story the way I remember living it, and I can only tell it the way I perceived it.

I recall that Rich used to always say, "Where you stand depends upon where you sit."

Lieutenant Colonel Robin Higgins, USMC (Ret)

Contents

Lieutenant Colonel William R. Higgins,
Official U.S. Marine Corps photo, 1987

Foreword

From my vantage point, Marine Colonel William "Rich" Higgins could only be described as a heroic Warrior who was the epitome of professionalism in all that he undertook in dedicated service to our great Nation and her ideals. He understood our Marine demands for extraordinary professional competence, and he strove to meet them. Rich also understood and lived by sound military leadership traits and principles. He always "led from the front" with moral courage and valor in both peace and war. Rich was both a man of action and of intellect, well-skilled in the "art of getting things done." He was bold without being rash in judgments or actions, and he was resolute in insuring that his people were trained for mission accomplishment to the extent practical. Above all, Rich Higgins possessed a strong sense of the great responsibility of command in carrying out missions and tasks.

In the early summer of 1987, then-Lieutenant Colonel Higgins was assigned to the United Nations as a member of the United Nations Truce Supervision Organization or UNTSO. After appropriate orientation and training, he was assigned as Chief of the U.N. military Observer Group in southern Lebanon. This group manned and occupied six observer posts in Lebanon along the Lebanese-Israeli armistice line. The unit also conducted patrolling operations and liaison activities in and around the hazardous area where U.N. peacekeeping forces operate. All military observers are unarmed. On 17 February 1988, Lieutenant

Colonel Higgins paid a call on an official from one of the principal Shi'ite organizations in the area known as Amal. While returning to his command post by jeep in a clearly marked and unarmed U.N. convoy, he was ruthlessly captured in a well-executed plan and held prisoner by radical Shi'ite group with links to the fundamentalist organization in Lebanon known as Hezbollah – the Party of God.

Rich Higgins was murdered at some point during his long months of captivity and was declared dead by the U.S. Marine Corps on 6 July 1990. Eighteen months later his body was dumped alongside of a road near Beirut. After confirmation by U.N. medical examiners, Colonel Higgins was brought home on 24 December 1991 to be with his God; his country he served so well; his Corps of Marines; his loving and incredibly courageous wife, Robin; his daughter and special love, Chrissy; his family and friends, and a Nation that would remember and pay tribute to his service.

Colonel Higgins' widow, Marine Lieutenant Colonel Robin Higgins, displayed enormous courage and faith throughout the long ordeal of her husband's cruel captivity and subsequent death. In *Patriot Dreams*, Robin shares with us the dramatic and intimate story of her struggle to free her husband and, after death, to bring his remains home to the country he loved.

In her inspiring personal account, Robin shares with us the Rich she knew and loved, their courtship and marriage, their love and dedication to the Marine Corps and to their country. We gain a greater understanding of where Robin finds the strength, faith and courage to handle enormous emotional stress and yet persevere in her relentless struggle to secure Rich's release. We also marvel at how she continued to serve as a Marine officer with dignity and distinction. We learn of her hopes and her fears, and her gratitude for those who helped and supported her.

With the utmost candor, our author tells of those officials and others in government and in the United Nations who, in her view, did not provide the help or the answers she desperately sought. An experienced media and public affairs officer in her own right, Robin provides examples of both accurate and irresponsible journalism. We see the potential for great harm to efforts undertaken to gain her husband's release when inaccurate and false statements are made. We also gain insights into the terrorist challenge we face and the difficulties encountered to defeat or neutralize them.

In summary, Robin Higgins has given us a powerful and moving book of love, loyalty, incredible courage, patriotism, emotional survival, relentless determination and faith. *Patriot Dreams* will hold lessons for all her readers.

The privilege of writing this foreword provides me the opportunity to comment on this wonderful and yet tragic story.

From the outset the abduction and imprisonment of Colonel Higgins to the time of his return, a group of dedicated civilian and military professionals operated relentlessly in America and overseas to bring Rich back safely and, after his murder, bring him home. Thousands of leads and reports were meticulously tracked down, analyzed and, as we say, run to ground and – not without some risk and danger. This group shall remain anonymous for obvious reasons, **but you know who you are**. You are indeed very special people, and you stayed with it even when there was little and then no hope to gain Rich's release while he was alive. In the end, we did not bring Rich home alive. You, like Rich, are a special breed, and the world is a safer place because of you.

For Rich Higgins, Colonel of Marines. Your courage and dedication in selfless service is and will be remembered. The magnificent *USS Higgins* (DDG-76) carries your name proudly. As long as men will dare to make a difference, the world will get better. You now have taken your place with that long line of soldiers of the sea who have served with distinction in peace and in war. Farewell my friend and – *Semper Fidelis*.

General A.M. Gray, Jr.
29th Commandant of the Marine Corps

William Richard Higgins,
Southern High School,
Louisville, Kentucky, 1963

Robin Lee Ross,
North Shore High School,
Glen Head, New York, 1968

Chapter 1
Sunray Is Missing

"I have felt the wind of madness pass over me."

— Baudelaire

**Nahariya, Israel
February 17, 1988
5:03 A.M.**

Lieutenant Colonel Rich Higgins was only a mile into his morning run when he spotted an armored patrol heading toward him. It was not flying the United Nations' flag, so he knew it was not his men. Rich had only been in Israel for a few weeks, but he had been a Marine for 20 years. The sight of heavily armed soldiers was not intimidating to the 43-year-old officer.

He kept jogging, eyes straight ahead, legs pumping fast and hard. If he kept moving, he reasoned, the patrol might ignore him and drive past. As it came closer, he saw it was an Israeli tank brigade returning from Lebanon. By now Rich was in their full view. The tanks slowed down, so he slowed down. They stopped, so he stopped. Just days before, an American civilian in Lebanon had been killed by Israeli soldiers like these. Driving by one of their convoys, the man had panicked and tried to drive past the soldiers. It was a very, very stupid thing to do in an area known for its Muslim terrorist suicide bombers. After the driver failed to heed several warning shots, the Israelis opened fire on the car, killing him instantly.

Rich wasn't a civilian. He knew the drill. He would remain still until the Israelis checked him out. If they asked for identification, he would show his U.N. identification card to the Israeli troops, and they would realize he was one of the peacekeepers. As the new chief of U.N. operations in the area, he had already been out on several training tours. Perhaps they would recognize him. They didn't.

Through binoculars, the tank commander scrutinized him intensely, looking for anything suspicious. He appeared to be like them. Rich's lean, tanned face, solid physique, and short hair were typical of the military men sent from Europe and North America to serve with the United Nations Truce Supervision Organization in Lebanon. But Rich showed none of the arrogance they often experienced from Westerners. He had no need for bravado. Rich was a professional soldier. He knew what to do in these situations: stand there, doing nothing confrontational, until they decided that he was no threat, and then resume his daily exercise run.

The approaching soldiers trained their weapons on him. The turret of the tank rotated, and the long, gray cannon dropped down until it pointed squarely at him. The tank's twin .50-caliber machine guns did the same. Rich knew that they could have vaporized him in the blink of an eye. Rich stared back, his eyes alert and aware. The soft lines around his eyes and mouth narrowed and hardened. With less than twenty yards between them, they stood there, Rich and the soldiers, studying each other, waiting for movement. Rich stood still and calm. It was not the first time he had looked down the loaded barrel of a tank's cannon.

The crackle of radio conversation signaled the end of the confrontation. They decided that Rich was harmless, and they waved him by. But in the Arab-Israeli conflict, no decision is without risk, and the tank's guns continued to track him until he turned and headed south, away from Lebanon.

Rich had started his morning run from Nahariya, the Israeli city that was home to the United Nations officers stationed in the area. It was morning and still tranquil. While he stood outside the house that morning, warming up for his run, he listened to the quiet. No planes, no jeeps, no gunfire, none of the sounds that would fill the rest of his day on the border of these two contentious countries. For a moment, it was peaceful.

He looked north toward southern Lebanon. The heat was already rising in waves from the ground, and the land across the border was a mirage: a placid, floating picture balanced on the horizon, daring him to run toward it. He knew that if he ran past Nahariya and into Lebanon that the picture would vanish when he got there. The calm was not real.

The face-off that morning with the Israeli tanks had demonstrated that there was nothing peaceful about the area around the Israeli-Lebanese border. It was the scene of the world's most inexplicable hatred, a bastion of fanaticism. The Israelis trained their guns on Rich because everyone is presumed to be the enemy, including unarmed men dressed in running shorts. In the tank commander's mind, Rich was a potential religious fanatic with a bomb strapped to his body. If they didn't take steps to rule out the prospect of his being a threat, he might detonate that bomb and kill them.

The confrontation typified the relations between the Arabs and the Israelis. Violence had become their way of life. Over the years, the roots of terror had found a stronghold in south Lebanon, where extreme Muslim factions hated not only Israel and its sympathizers, but each other as well. Every opponent was hard fought with a maniacal fury. To most Westerners, the fighting style of the Shi'ite Muslims appeared to be without strategy, form, or reason. It was, in fact, meticulously planned guerrilla warfare. Even when the fighting seemed to subside, it never disappeared. Instead, it lay dormant under the surface, stewing and churning until it was set off again.

As allies of the hated Israelis, Americans in Lebanon faced certain danger. Rich suffered no delusions about his safety. He understood that service in a U.N. agency didn't provide him any protection. When several Scandinavian U.N. workers were kidnapped, their status as neutral, unarmed humanitarian workers didn't ensure their safety. Rich could have pulled in horns and led a low-key life, but that would have been inconceivable for him. He had no intention of doing any less than his full duty — or any less than his Australian predecessor, Lieutenant Colonel Ewen Cameron, whose command Rich described as a "tight ship on a steady course."

Rich had not come to the Israeli-Lebanese border to fight, but rather to ease tensions. He was on a one-year tour with the United Nations, unaccompanied by his family. As a Marine, it was important for Rich to gain valuable field experience. The Corps was, after all, the branch of the armed services relied upon for skilled combat soldiers. Marine officers like Rich actively sought out opportunities to learn, lead, and command forces in the thick of the action. Like Rich, officers often accepted an assignment that took them outside of the Corps if it offered the chance be in the field.

As a member of the United Nations Truce Supervision Organization (UNTSO), Rich was a Marine assigned to the United Nations. Formed in 1948, UNTSO was an arm of the U.N. that supervised the truce called for by the United Nations Security Council after the first conflict between Arabs and Jews over the formation of Israel. Its first commander had been an American. Since then its military observers remained as a peacekeeping force to monitor the armistice agreement between Israel and its Arab neighbors.

Rich had been warned by the intelligence officer of a local militia that there was a price on his head. Nevertheless, he was adamant about doing his job to the best of his ability. He knew that in 1948, the UNTSO's first commanding officer had been an American, and he felt that it was important for the United States to fulfill its regular turn in the UNTSO leadership rotation.

In order to emphasize their role as mediators between warring factions, all UNTSO officers and enlisted men were unarmed. Their only protection was the degree to which the parties in conflict cooperated with the U.N.'s declaration for peace. They had no actual power to prevent a breach of the truce or to enforce any decisions, but their very presence acted as a deterrent to violating the cease-fire.

The mission of UNTSO, then, was peace in the Middle East. Although it was a relatively small operation, UNTSO drew its 300 men from nineteen countries. Besides Israel and Lebanon, it had operations in

Egypt, Jordan, and Syria, with each territory assigned a group of officers and men known as an observer group. After training and observing for three months in Egypt, followed by another three months in Lebanon, Rich was appointed chief of Observer Group Lebanon (OGL) on January 8, 1988. OGL maintained six observation towers staffed by two-man teams. Ground patrols moved between the observation posts. The job of the observers was to report violations in the security zone, such as overflights by the Israeli Air Force, incursions by ground troops, and terrorist activities. OGL also had several two-man liaison teams whose job was to meet with other friendly forces. The largest of these was the United Nations Interim Force in Lebanon (UNIFIL), an armed force six thousand strong. They were on call in case the peacekeepers were directly threatened by the warring factions.

As chief of OGL, Rich was in charge of a multi-national contingent of 75 men. He was also the senior American officer out of the seventy or so American military men operating in other UNTSO observer groups and of the fifteen other American troops working for UNTSO in Lebanon. His job was twofold: to command his observer group and to ensure the welfare of not only the officers in OGL, but also the welfare of all United States officers in UNTSO. While other observers manned the observation posts, Rich had the responsibility of traveling throughout the area, visiting all of the OGL towers, ground patrols, and liaison teams. It was his duty to guarantee that OGL headquarters in Naqoura, Lebanon, and the six towers worked together like a well-oiled military machine.

For Rich, any successful military operation relied on the readiness, training, and quality of its soldiers. He drilled and trained his troops in an endless drive for technical and tactical expertise. Every man at OGL was under his charge, and in order to protect them, he had to make sure they were proficient in every aspect of security. He was obsessed with the challenge of preparing his men to handle the brutal, frenzied warfare of the Arab-Israeli conflict. They needed to know how to work together as a team to soothe tempers of the rival groups. The demands he placed on his soldiers were no less than those he placed on himself. No sacrifice was too great to secure the success of the mission.

There was no doubt that Lebanon was a dangerous place. Driving anywhere in the southern Lebanese countryside was even more perilous, especially for an American. Rich knew the risks, but they came with his job. He was a hands-on commander, and needed to be out among his men. A leader by Marine training, he had been indoctrinated in the Corps' philosophy of activist leadership early in his career. It was impossible for Rich to think of simply issuing orders from his office at Naqoura. Peace would not exist of its own free will; it was up to the United Nations forces to build it, guard it, and pass it on. Thinking, acting, and accomplishing was Rich's style of command. His men saw him sweating under the Lebanese sun, watching for signs of trouble from a tower, pushing for good relations between Israel and Lebanon. He worked with them but put more on the line. He led from the front, and his troops followed him. He was a soldier just like them, and they were dedicated to him.

They didn't mind the preparation and drills that Rich put them through. Although they were unarmed, the officers at OGL knew they worked in a battlefield every day. Radical Muslim groups had killed United Nations officers before. Only months earlier, in October 1987, a U.N. soldier from Nepal had been shot. When the ambulance came for him, the Lebanese Army fired on that, too. It was not the U.N.'s battle, but they had become a fixture of the war, an enemy to the most extreme factions simply by virtue of their longstanding presence. In Rich's mind, any person was in danger as soon as he crossed the border into Lebanon. The U.N. officers understood Rich's style of command. It made them better soldiers, and they trusted him, just as his troops in Vietnam had. At the end of the day, they were confident that he would lead them safely home.

His task was not easy. Rich knew that even when the air seemed clear and still, there was still that rancorous undercurrent running an erratic line beneath the ground, ready to spark another fiery confrontation. When he rode through the Lebanese countryside, he knew the risks. In letters home, he wrote about the dangers he faced daily, but he also wrote of his confidence, knowing that despite all the fighting, peace would somehow prevail. Rich was strangely comfortable in that sort of environment, in places where most people would never venture, in places marred by conflict and misunderstanding. They were places where his leadership had the biggest impact.

Rich and his men were there to make peace happen, and on some future day, he would be able to stand at an observation tower, surrounded by calm, and breathe deeply, smelling the clean, crisp air, the lingering odors of smoke and gunfire gone. No plane would be diving in attack. Guns would not be threatening his men.

To Rich, fighting was an ugly thing. He did not enjoy war. He had seen how it could tear apart soldiers, families, and entire countries. Rich had risked his life fighting in Vietnam, believing amid all the chaos and death that there was a sincere mission. Although Lebanon was not the battlefields of Vietnam, the intensity was there. Rich and the other U.N. officers were working in a place where war was a way of life. If his officers weren't ready and didn't know the dangers, they could be killed. Or they could be maimed forever, living the rest of their lives with constant reminders of how a war that they were trying to stop had changed them.

He had seen his soldiers get hurt before. In Vietnam, they were riddled with bullets and sent home in wheelchairs, missing arms and legs. Others were thrown into the air by the blasts of land mines, their eyes and ears burned so badly that they would never see or hear again. When they lay on the ground, wounded and delirious, Rich was often the one who held them until a helicopter came. There was something about him that was reassuring. There was a quiet compassion, a genuine concern that soothed the scared and wounded. He had watched hearts and lungs pumping the last bit of life through their torn bodies. He listened while they prayed or cried, trying to will his own strength into their bodies, even when it was futile. In Lebanon, he thought, it should not be that way. There should be no casualties of peace.

As in Vietnam, the boundaries of fighting along the Israeli-Lebanese border were not clearly marked. There was no completely safe space, even for the peacekeepers, in a region where peace is more often an ideal than a reality. On January 12, 1988, four days after he had taken charge of OGL, one of his officers was killed and another wounded by a roadside bomb. Australian Captain Peter McCarthy had been on a routine patrol with a Canadian officer, Major Gilbert Cote, en route to the Lebanese village of Shama. The two men were scheduled to make a radio report at 1:45 in the afternoon. After no contact was received, Rich directed that an intensive ground search be started. Two Lebanese civilians told a team of officers that they had seen a U.N. vehicle go by and heard an explosion shortly thereafter. When the officers found Major

Cote, he was wounded but able to tell them that McCarthy was dead — the victim of a land mine explosion. One-and-a-half kilometers up the road, they found the car and McCarthy.

Every person in OGL was shaken. Rich mounted an immediate investigation. "He said he was determined that victims of terrorism like McCarthy would not be blamed simply because they were unlucky enough to have been in harm's way while performing their duty," wrote Rona M. Fields in *The Washington Post*.

Unlike the U.S., which recognized the high potential for danger, several other countries who assigned soldiers to UNTSO allowed their families to accompany them to Lebanon. Families who believed their loved ones were a part of a safe, unarmed force were now faced with the grim, daunting reality of terrorism.

For Rich, the death of one of his men was hard to accept, and with the pain of the loss came doubts. He had been their commander for only four days. Had they been properly trained? Were they aware of all the correct security procedures? What could he do to ensure it wouldn't happen again? At that moment, he didn't know, but he couldn't let his men see his uncertainty.

After the death of Captain McCarthy, morale sank fast among the OGL team members. Their optimism and enthusiasm were waning, and some were becoming leery of serving. Rich saw the hesitation in their step and the fear on their faces. It was his job to rekindle OGL's spirits. He would remind the soldiers what the mission was about, make them remember the promise they had made to their countries and the United Nations.

Rich called the troops and their families together. Almost two hundred people filled a hall near headquarters. He asked them to join hands. Rich told them they needed to create a support system of soldiers and families bound together as tightly as they now held onto one another. Each person in the room was connected to all the others by a military lineage, he told them, a long line of soldiers and their families who had given their lives and loves for peace and honor. Whatever his fate, the soldier's dedication to the mission made him forever a part of that line.

His men understood. In order to endure tragedy, a soldier drew strength from his military brethren. For the troops of OGL, Rich would be the source of that strength. It would flow from him. His own connection to the military was thick as blood, and the Corps was his family. The thoughts and movements, sounds and pulse of other Marines were his own. Even from his military residence in Nahariya, he heard, in the back of his mind, the crisp notes of reveille that blasted through the barracks at Camp Lejeune, North Carolina, every morning. He felt the rhythmic thump of soldiers marching across a field in the sticky summer heat of Quantico, Virginia. They lined up in formation, young Marines standing tense and wide-eyed while drill sergeants barked orders at them.

Twenty years earlier, in 1967, Rich had stood on that field. He was 22 years old, just out of college and headed for Vietnam. His drill sergeant paced in front of the line, shouting commands through the pouring rain. Suddenly he stopped an inch from Rich's face. Staring the boy squarely in the eye, he called Rich, "Marine."

That day in 1967, he later told his troops, was his initiation into the brotherhood of the Corps, and he remembered it as the most meaningful event of his life. Now, twenty years later, on a roadside in Israel, someone had violated that kinship by taking the life of a fellow soldier. Even worse, they had killed like cowards and without remorse. The terrorists' defiance of UNTSO's mission had become clear to OGL, and their duties were all the more important. If the U.N. crawled away with its tail between its legs, a band of Muslim fanatics hiding somewhere in the Bekaa Valley would have won, and a good soldier would have died in vain.

Over the following weeks, Rich saw the enthusiasm return. His men were from different parts of the world, yet they had heard his message. It was universal, these soldiers' devotion to one another, and Rich knew it. Their chief had come through once again. He was their motivator, mentor, and fellow soldier. But most important of all, he was their leader.

Although the mission was back on track, Rich couldn't help but worry about the future. Would it happen again? He and his men could watch from the towers and monitor the fighting zones, but could they alone prevent another terrorist act? He knew it would also take the cooperation of Lebanese factions. When Rich took command of OGL, he believed that part of his job was to work with all the Israeli and Lebanese factions to prevent further fighting. The U.N. troops were, after all, working for peace. How would it ever be achieved if they didn't take measures to establish active communication between the peacekeepers and among the fighters?

Rich made sure both sides saw that he wouldn't be a behind-the-scenes commander. From the beginning, he maintained a high- visibility professional profile, letting the Israeli and Lebanese forces know that he would be an active peacekeeper. In a letter dated November 28, 1987, he wrote:

> *I faced the first obstacle yesterday when I had to drive alone through the enclave to pick up my patrol mate. There was some initial concern regarding an American alone in the area controlled by Amal and Hezbollah — but I insisted I would not begin compromising now. With the exception of small arms fire — which wasn't directed at me — the trip was uneventful, however. I think I passed the first test, and word is out that the new American isn't afraid — so one day at a time. (By the way, I was afraid, but I hope it didn't show. One would be foolish not to be. It's like that feeling you get just before you have to appear before a group to speak — but it goes away.)*

Rich had the responsibility to prove that he would come and go wherever and whenever his mission demanded it. The Chief of OGL would not be intimidated. He rode across borders in his Jeep, met with leaders, and went to the scene of any attack. He visited Shi'ite extremist strongholds, walking among some of the most dangerous men in the world. In order to see every road where there had been a car bomb in the last three months, he spent days at a time in areas where no other American was allowed. That was his job, and he didn't shrink from it. The letter from November 28th continued:

> *I am now the only American who travels the area of operations. I've been in most of the areas, including Hezbollah villages, and I'm still safe. I've been on every road where there was a car bomb in the last three months, and I still believe that no one is irrational enough to take on the U.N. Chief of OGL — who has world backing and*

is unarmed. It is an experience you wouldn't believe. I won't bore you with the stories (yet), but today we must have heard around 2,000 rounds of fire. But none of it was really directed at me.

Although Rich frequently crossed the line of fire, he was never confrontational. He befriended Lebanese citizens who were willing to talk with him. He described one of these meetings this way:

I had a fascinating three-hour meeting with five leaders of the Shi'ites, Amal, a professor from Beirut, and some local people. We had a discussion of American foreign policy, the geo-political dilemma of the Mideast, and local Lebanese situation that any M.I.T. professor on the subject would have given anything to attend. It was the most fascinating discussion I have ever had on the subject and had to reach down to all of my knowledge on the subject to keep even — because, of course, America was the focus of the attack. But I believe we left with a mutual respect. The best part was that I was allowed to leave — I'm kidding, but I always keep that in the back of my mind. That is the biggest fear.

Rich knew that the ordinary Lebanese people were concerned about their own safety, and, as with his soldiers, he gave them hope. Eventually, he told them, people would walk freely through Lebanon without the threat of attack. At night, families would be able to sleep soundly, undisturbed by the bark of machine guns. They would look out of their windows and see the deep night sky, undefiled by smoke and streaks of distant tracer fire. That was the peace that Rich envisioned: a safe, cool quiet allowing people to sleep through the night; one where children play without fear of gunfire; a peace where men and women could walk the streets without looking over their shoulders at each corner or flinch at every city noise.

His work attracted the attention of a band of Shi'ite Muslims known as Amal. One of a handful of terrorist splinter groups in Lebanon, Amal was considered the most moderate of the violent factions. Its leader was Nabih Berri, Lebanon's Minister of Justice. Unlike other

Shi'ite Muslims, such as the radical Hezbollah,[1] the more-moderate Amal did not lash out directly against the United Nations or the United States.

The Hezbollah and the Amal are opposing factions in Lebanon. The Hezbollah is a radical Shi'ite Muslim faction dedicated to establishing an Iranian-style Islamic republic in Lebanon and removing all non-Islamic influences from the area. They are strongly anti-Western and violently anti-Israel. Their activities are closely allied with, and often directed by Iran, which provides Hezbollah with substantial amounts of financial, diplomatic, and political aid, as well as training, weapons, and explosives. Their several thousand members operate out of the southern suburbs of Beirut and the Bekaa Valley. According to the Department of State, the Hezbollah were known or suspected to have been involved in numerous anti-U.S. attacks, including the suicide truck-bombing of the U.S. Embassy and U.S. Marine barracks in Beirut in October 1983 and the U.S. Embassy annex in Beirut in September 1984. They also hijacked TWA Flight 847 in 1985. These terrorists were also responsible for the kidnapping and incarceration of most or all U.S. and other Western hostages in Lebanon.

Until the mid-1990s, when the Hezbollah started pushing hard for dominance in Lebanon, Amal forces controlled most of southern Lebanon. Amal avoided attacks on U.N. troops in Lebanon, whom they saw as a buffer between themselves and the Israelis. Amal did, however, launch strikes against Hezbollah, because both had strongholds in southern Lebanon and often fought for control of the area.

After Australian Capt. Peter McCarthy was killed, Rich arranged a meeting with Abdel Majeed Saleh, an Amal senior political official, to discuss what could be done to prevent future terrorist acts like the roadside bombing. He wanted Saleh and his men to help OGL combat terrorism and deal with any unexpected hostile events. Rich had hoped there would be no casualties of peace while he was in Lebanon, but in the first month of his command, there had already been one. He was determined to keep it from happening again.

---

[1] The Hizb'Allah, or "Army of God," which operates in Lebanon is often an umbrella for the Party of God, the Islamic Jihad, the Revolutionary Justice Organization, and the Organization for the Oppressed of the Earth. The spelling "Hezbollah" will be used here because it is the spelling used in so many news reports quoted here.

Saleh, who had met with Rich once before, agreed to meet with him again on February 17, 1988, a little over a month after the bombing. Rich was optimistic about talking with Saleh. He had jokingly called the meeting "a talk with the bad guys," since the Amal were often a part of the problem. Now it seemed they might be a part of the solution. They would cooperate with any efforts that prevented action by their Hezbollah enemies. In the past few months, terrorist attacks affecting the U.N. had increased. The murder of Captain McCarthy was followed by the early February abductions in Lebanon of two U.N. employees, one Swedish and the other Norwegian.

If terrorism continued to escalate, unarmed peacekeepers might be forced to pull out of the area. Amal wanted them to stay. Without the U.N., Amal was faced with the potential of a war incited by the more radical Muslims. Extremists like Hezbollah were backed by Iran, who provided them with continuous access to money, weapons, and training. With this strong support, Hezbollah could use any means they wanted to achieve their goal of turning Lebanon into a fundamentalist Muslim state. In an environment unsupervised by the U.N., they would be even more able to see their vision realized. While the peacekeeping troops couldn't stop terrorism altogether, at least their presence drew a line in the sand for Hezbollah. Without that line, they would observe no boundaries, political or moral. Allying themselves with the U.N., then, was beneficial to Amal since the peacekeepers' presence helped sustain the truce between rivals.

On the morning of February 17, 1988, Rich was, as usual, the first of the U.N. officers to rise. He showered, shaved, and trimmed his moustache. It had more gray now than when he arrived in the Middle East a relatively short time ago.

He noticed through the bathroom window that the sky was still filled with clouds. The seasonal rains had just begun, turning the roads to mud and slowing down operations. Rich would have to remember to allow extra time to drive to the meeting with Saleh. Roads would be in poor condition, full of potholes and cut with deep, treacherous ruts.

Rising before the others gave him time to make the coffee and think. Today would be hectic, with work at his headquarters in Naqoura, and then the meeting with Saleh. Early morning was the only time of the day when he could let his mind wander. Rich remembered his childhood in Kentucky, waking every morning to the crackle of bacon and the smell of biscuits and country ham. In Israel, he would have to settle for coffee and thoughts of home.

Rich knew that he had only four months left on his U.N. tour. Soon he would be back in America. Originally, he was assigned to leave in mid-summer, but had received permission to return home early to attend his daughter Chrissy's high school graduation.

His hastened departure made the meeting with Saleh even more important. Rich didn't have much time left at OGL, and he wanted to leave knowing that the sacrifices and work of his men had paid off. Improved relations, or maybe even an alliance, between U.N. forces and a Shi'ite group like Amal would certainly be progress.

Then he could go home to his family in Virginia. Perhaps he would return a colonel, as well. Three days earlier, Rich had called to wish his wife Robin, then a major in the Marines, a happy Valentine's Day. He learned that his selection board was in session, and the promotion seemed certain. His dream of becoming a colonel and commanding his own regiment might well come true soon. He imagined the ceremony: standing proudly at attention while his friend, General Al Gray, Commandant of the Marine Corps, pinned his silver eagles on his shoulders. His family would be there watching.

He wished his father could be there, too, but he knew that would be impossible. Billy Higgins was sick, dying of advanced heart disease in a Louisville, Kentucky, hospital. For the next three days, Rich would be busy traveling inside Lebanon and unable to contact his family. He worried that his father might die without his even knowing. He put the thought out of his mind.

Finishing his coffee, he rose from the breakfast table. It was already 5:30 A.M., and he needed to be at headquarters by 6:00 A.M. He took off his wedding band and emptied his pockets. OGL headquarters was across the Lebanese border in Naqoura, and no personal effects were ever taken into Lebanon. U.N. soldiers carried only their U.N. and national identification cards in their pockets.

The drive from Nahariya to Naqoura was seventeen kilometers. The road they would travel was contested between the Amal militia and the more radical, Iran-backed Hezbollah movement, which in 1986 had launched rocket attacks against the UNTSO forces. U.N. soldiers made the trip in United Nations' Jeep Cherokees, which were marked with black, two-foot-high "U.N." letters and symbols on the sides, hood, and doors. A blue U.N. flag flew from the radio antenna. UNTSO troops, including Rich, took every measure possible to ensure that everyone knew they were with the United Nations.

For Westerners, wearing the blue U.N. beret with the uniform of their country signaled to others that they were peacekeepers. Soldiers from countries which, like the United States, had close ties with Israel faced added danger of terrorist attack. On Rich's standard issue U.S. Marine uniform, the normal red, white, and blue of the small American flag patch on his shoulder was sewn with thread that was the same dark green as his sweater and pants. Others had suggested that he cover the flag entirely. One of the officers in his command, Canadian Major Vern McKeen, offered Rich some stick-on Canadian flag patches that could be used to cover his American flag if they were confronted by Hezbollah troublemakers. If they were stopped, the Canadian patches could save Rich's life. He refused to wear them. He told Major McKeen, "Vern, with respect to you and your country, if I get into a tight situation I'll do it wearing my country's flag. I won't hide behind another nation's flag."[2]

Once at headquarters, Rich began his daily routine. He checked the officers on duty, making sure they knew their tasks for the day. There were no immediate problems that needed his attention, just some routine paperwork that had piled up on his desk. After spending the morning at Naqoura, Rich would leave to make the ten-mile drive north to Tyre, the site of his meeting with Saleh. The trip and the meeting with Saleh would take most of the afternoon.

Before Rich left, he met his friend, Maj. Mike Sullivan, in the parking lot. As operations team leader, Mike was responsible for

---

[2] Major Vern McKeen letter to then-Commandant of the Marne Corps, General Al M. Gray, Jr., March 18, 1988.

ensuring communications were maintained with any member of OGL who was traveling through dangerous areas. Mike and his team monitored and controlled movement through the use of checkpoints. As a U.N. vehicle passed each checkpoint along the road, the soldiers there radioed back to the headquarters, confirming their status and position. Rich was, as always, concerned about safety. He asked his friend to be especially watchful that day. Mike knew about Rich's meeting in Tyre and knew how Rich had been anticipating it. The two officers shared an apartment in Nahariya. Mike had seen Rich awake late at night, taking notes, going over files about Amal, brainstorming on ways OGL and Amal could work together. When Mike recalled the scene in the parking lot, he said, "There was a feeling between us that this day would be different — almost like a sense of predestination. I can't explain it, but there was electricity in our conversation. We both sensed fear, but neither of us could do anything about it. I honestly believe that Rich knew his fate on this date."

After he left Mike, Rich met with the two-man liaison team that would accompany him into southern Lebanon. Since security regulations required that UNTSO troops always travel in a convoy, they would ride in a Jeep ahead of Rich. No one in their right mind traveled alone in Lebanon unless there was a compelling need to do so.

In addition to the convoy, U.N. troops followed extensive security procedures when they traveled. Before they left, Rich and the liaison team checked their radios to make sure they were operating clearly. The two Jeeps needed not only communication with the headquarters, but also clear transmission with each other. They tested the radios several times. The liaison team called Rich, and he returned a call to them, using the call sign given to the OGL chief, "Sunray."

Rich was compulsive about security procedures such as radio checks, especially when the weather was as bad as it was that morning. The trip north into Lebanon was not very long, just fifteen kilometers. With the rain and mud, visibility was low, and he knew that if they lost sight of each other, the radios would keep them in contact.

The Lebanese city of Tyre was reached by driving north from Naqoura along a coastal highway. On the way, Rich and the liaison team stopped to visit one of the two-man observation posts. After seeing that everything was running smoothly, the convoy continued north. Rich watched the Jeep in front of him plow through mud and dive into potholes. He tried to avoid the holes that nearly bogged down the lead Jeep, but still had to push and grind his way through the deep ruts. By now, both of the white Jeep Cherokees were covered with mud up to the doors. The U.N. symbols were splattered and the windows coated with a hazy brown muck. It was slow going, but Rich had allowed them plenty of time. They weren't expected in Tyre until noon.

During the meeting, he found that Saleh did indeed want to work with OGL. Rich's ideas about the Amal leader had been right. Saleh was willing to participate with any plan that curtailed Hezbollah activity. He spoke of help and change and cooperation and was not like other leaders Rich had encountered in Lebanon. After traveling among the extremist camps, his picture of a Muslim commander was stark. The men he met were sullen and brooding, giving Rich the feeling that they moved in constant shadow. When Rich tried to make eye contact, they shifted their eyes, their expressions enigmatic and unreadable.

With Saleh, Rich sensed a bit more openness. Rich could see into his eyes. While the two leaders talked, the other two officers from Rich's convoy waited outside, smoking and talking to Saleh's men. They watched the rain, hoping that it would subside. If the sun came out, the mud would harden, and the drive home would be easier.

By the end of the meeting, the weather had worsened. It was just after two o'clock in the afternoon when Rich and his two-man liaison team started their drive back down the coastal highway toward Naqoura. Visibility was even poorer than it had been earlier. At Ras el-Ain, about four miles south of Tyre, the convoy passed a crossroad that led to the Shi'ite-controlled Palestinian refugee camp of Rashidiyah. Just beyond the crossroad, the lead Jeep went around a bend. At nearly every curve, the wheels of the Jeep ground into the sides of the ruts, almost sticking and then spitting up mud. Rich had learned to drive far enough behind them to avoid the spray from the back wheels. We remained close enough for visual contact, though, because the vehicles were required to keep each other in sight at all times. Even though Sunray made his own calls to headquarters at each checkpoint, the liaison team reported his status as well when they radioed back.

When the lead Jeep rounded the bend, Rich was still behind the curve, temporarily out of view. After the road straightened, the two men looked back to make sure Rich was still behind them. The rear window was hazy, dripping with muddy water, but they could see that his Jeep had not yet appeared.

They turned back for him, thinking the car had stalled or was stuck in the mud. They knew that even in a driving rain, it wasn't safe to be stopped on the side of the road in Lebanon.

When they got to the car, Rich wasn't in it. The door was open, and the engine was still. There was no sign of a struggle and no bullet holes. They looked around for Rich, hoping that maybe he left the car to help someone, but he was nowhere in sight. One of the officers jumped back into his Jeep and keyed the radio's microphone. Back at headquarters, Major Mike Sullivan heard the dreaded message rasp through the loudspeaker: "Sunray is missing!"

Chapter 2

Hearts Divided

The Pentagon
February 17, 1988
9:00 A.M.

My boss, Dan Howard, the Pentagon's top spokesman, had called for a meeting to begin the day. This was standard operating procedure at least a couple of times a week. Dan, a professional information officer for years, was insistent on good communication amongst ourselves, on making sure that each of us had the same information and were playing from the same deck. None of the people in the room had any way to anticipate the crisis which would soon engulf us all so personally.

These meetings were a way for all of us to catch up and sometimes to catch our breath, to learn what the others were doing, to get the latest news. On February 17th, we were helping Dan to prepare for one of his biweekly press conferences. We all had the responsibility to be accurate and consistent at every moment. As Public Affairs officers for the Pentagon, we interacted with the media on a daily, sometimes hourly basis. Accurate information is critically important in the modern world. Without it, none of us could be effective in our jobs. Those of us in the Pentagon knew then what newcomers to the Internet are now learning — that there are huge quantities of information everywhere. Some of it is reliable fact; some is opinion; and much of it is deliberately false or misleading. Sifting through it all requires intelligence, training, and good judgment.

As military press professionals, we were all trained on how to properly handle the information we had. Yet sifting through the reams of information every day was not easy. It was often difficult to decide what was important and what wasn't; what could be released and what, for national security reasons, could not. If we misjudged, or if we overlooked a small piece of critical information, the effects could be devastating. Since we worked in such high-pressure jobs, spending an hour or so at a staff-only meeting every couple of days was a nice break for us. During the meeting, at least we could relax a bit and enjoy the company of our fellow professionals.

There were six of us at the meeting that day: Dan Howard, his two deputies, and their three military assistants. Dan, a stocky, graying, kindly looking public servant, was relatively new to the job, having been brought in by Frank Carlucci, the new Secretary of Defense. But the rest of us had worked together for quite a while. In the short time we had come to know our new boss, however, we developed a keen respect for him and for his ability to analyze the news and deal with crises wisely. Relative rank and the power that rank holds were not important to him. He treated us all as professionals. We liked his attitude.

While waiting for Dan to convene the meeting, we "old hands" stood around in the outer office, sipping the watery coffee that seemed to be the mainstay of every official meeting and chatting about some silly story that had been in the Early Bird that morning. The Early Bird was the Pentagon clipping service, a compilation of news articles from all over the world of interest to the Defense Department. Distributed around the Pentagon, the State Department, and the rest of Washington government at 6:30 each morning, it set the tone for activity and water-cooler conversation inside the Beltway. We six were among the very first in Washington to get copies of the Early Bird; it drove our agenda as well.

It often took Dan a few minutes to get meetings under way. He was constantly busy, attending to things that needed his opinion, needed to be signed. He preferred dealing with breaking news stories, as we all did, but his military assistant, Commander Bill Harlow, kept piling paperwork, briefing books, and decision memoranda in front of him. Dan would usually try to quickly dispose of such material in the morning before "all hell broke loose." Every once in a while something would require more attention and time than he had planned for it, and the next scheduled appointment would have to wait.

As we gathered outside his office for the meetings, we'd look in. If he were still pulling papers from the vast pile called his in-box, we knew we still had a few more minutes to chat. When he was ready, he'd raise his eyes briefly in our direction. We were military professionals, and his eye contact was the signal we'd need to immediately shuffle in and take our seats at the long table opposite the desk. This day Dan did not sit at the table with us, but at his desk facing us. In retrospect, it was somewhat uncharacteristic of this hands-on, personable professional.

At 9:15 A.M., Dan started the meeting. His normal exercise was to go around the room, giving each person an opportunity to report on items which we believed the media would want and need to know about that day. He began by turning to the always-taciturn Fred Hoffman, a veteran newsman-turned-government spokesman.

A few minutes into his review, the "bat phone" (our nickname) rang. It was a special, direct link to the Secretary of Defense. It rings with a special, shrill sound. Secretary Carlucci and Dan, being quite close, used it quite frequently to keep in total synch with each other for press and public encounters, without having to bother or go through lines of secretaries and military assistants. The interruption was not unusual. We were all alert for the signs that the call might be sensitive, our indication to rise and move back out to the outer office so the men could have privacy. Dan was intent on what the voice on the other end was saying. We knew instinctively it was bad news, and we were each trying to interpret from Dan's hardened poker face just how bad it was going to be. We all knew how treacherous the times were and how so many things could go wrong in so many places. Sadly, we'd all been there for too many calls bearing bad news.

We were silent. Each of us envisioned all kinds of scenarios unfolding. We didn't have time for prayer, but silently I think each of us was preparing for battle. It's not just that we wanted to be prepared for another crisis, for crisis management was our job, and we reveled in it. Rather, we all knew that whenever that special phone rang, lives could be in grave danger — or already lost.

We waited silently, trying to guess what was happening. A few of us glanced at each other, questions clearly in our eyes if not on our lips. I was the junior military assistant and the only woman there. I wanted to do what the others were doing, to show that I was just as good, just as ready. Certainly it would be something newsworthy.

Within a few minutes, the phone call ended. Dan hadn't said much other than "I see" and "Uh huh." He hung up the phone abruptly and looked directly at Bill Harlow, knowing that his trusted military assistant would know what to do without wasted words.

With no preamble or waver in his voice, Dan stated, "We've got a problem. A Marine lieutenant colonel working with the U.N. was just taken hostage in Lebanon."

The air in the room became thick and oppressive. I felt as if I had been dropped into a murky bog, and I struggled to keep my head above water. I felt everyone's eyes on me, but I couldn't return their gaze. In the now-frozen moment, I watched chunks of coffee creamer float in an oily patch in my styrofoam cup. They meandered in circles, bumping one another, careening off in new paths, always a circle, no beginning, no ending.

I remember listening to the ticking of the huge clock on the wall. It resembled those old-fashioned schoolroom clocks. Its stark white face and oversized black numbers loomed on the wall above Dan's head. The second hand seemed to have stopped, but the ticking grew louder and louder, reverberating through the stunned silence of my fellow press officers.

Bill mustered up the courage to say to Dan, "Boss, Robin's husband Rich is a Marine lieutenant colonel in Lebanon."

I heard him and said numbly, "It's Rich."

Bill faced me and said quietly, "Now let's not jump to conclusions. It might be someone else."

"No," I said. "He is the only Marine lieutenant colonel there. It is Rich."

Other than Dan, everyone at the table knew that the man who had been kidnapped was my husband, Rich. I knew it too. Rich was the only Marine lieutenant colonel in Lebanon. There was no possibility that it could have been anyone else.

The coffee creamer had slowed its frenzied circling in my cup. As I stared at it, one of the larger white clumps triggered memories of my wedding day and the joy Rich and I shared, believing that we could overcome everything. For some reason I found myself trying to remember the name of the last movie that Rich, I, and his daughter Chrissy had gone to. I rubbed my upper lip, remembering the tickle of his mustache the last time we kissed goodbye. Did he still have it? I forgot. I heard Rich calling to me, but I couldn't hear what he was saying.

Everything Rich and I had ever done together, all the words we'd said and had yet to say, roared through my head, filling the awful silence that had saturated the room.

Perhaps it was only half a minute that passed. Then Dan looked at me, too. For some reason I still don't understand, it was his look that brought me back to the room, that reminded me I needed to do something.

Dan knew that Rich was a Marine and knew that he was stationed somewhere in the Middle East, but he hadn't known where. Now he knew. Within that agonizing half-minute, Dan had taken in the horrified eyes turned my way and understood that in the second it had taken him to make his announcement, he had changed my life.

All he could say was "I'm sorry." Sorry that what he had said might have sounded callous.

Time started again. Everyone in the room clustered around me, offering their support and sympathy. Still standing in the same position I was while waiting to receive Dan's statement — was it only moments ago? — I think I remember acknowledging their offers of help with a nod and a touch of my hand. I still couldn't say anything. It wasn't that I wanted to or didn't want to. Talking just didn't occur to me. Words didn't seem important then. There was so much to feel, so much to do.

Everyone started gathering their notes from the conference table. Maybe I gathered mine a bit more slowly. I heard talk from a distance and couldn't really distinguish what it was they were saying. I knew we all had extraordinary work to do. The abduction of my husband was major news. The U.N. peacekeeping force and the United States of America had been set upon. And we were the press officers who would now begin to influence the knowledge the world would have of this event.

Our meeting was certainly over, but our real work was just starting. It was going to be tough. This time it was one of our own we needed to report on, and we had to deal with it.

Someone swung open the door leading out of Dan's office into the front office and the long public affairs corridor. The public affairs center in the "E" ring of the Pentagon, called the Correspondents' Corridor, was set up to allow for the easiest communication paths between all affected parties. Each of the deputy assistant secretaries and their military assistants had their places near Dan so we could immediately be notified of breaking news. Down the corridor were the offices of the Pentagon press corps: the network news staffs, major newspapers, AP, UPI, Reuters, and others. And directly across from them was a huge open bay of cluttered desks of military public affairs officers from each service to provide them with what they needed. When something happened, we all needed quick access to each other.

As we filed out from Dan's office, we met Fred Francis of NBC, David Martin of CBS, Bob Zelnick of ABC, Carl Rochelle of CNN, and Charlie Aldinger of Reuters. They'd left their offices and were milling anxiously in the corridor, desperate to speak to Dan Howard and to me. They'd heard the news of Rich's capture even before we had.

Most of these reporters were my friends. We worked along the same corridor, dealt with the same information, and saw each other constantly. Some of them had even worked with Rich before his Middle East tour took him out of the Pentagon. As I left Dan's office and found myself in their midst, I knew they had heard the kidnapped victim was Rich. Their eyes bored in on me. Even if they hadn't known me, this was still news. They immediately started asking questions, but they were unusually gentle.

"Robin, is it true?" one asked.

"Robin, can I ask you a few questions about Rich?" another said.

I couldn't talk, not then. I needed to plan a strategy. I needed to contact Chrissy. I needed Rich.

I brushed past them all and hurried to my little cubicle to try and gather my thoughts. I heard Dan ask the press to give us a minute to figure out what we were going to do. Good plan, I thought. That's what I needed to do.

I heard the press leave, hushed whispers echoing down the long hall, bouncing off the empty walls. Although it was their job to find out and report what was going on, they knew me, and many of them knew Rich. This was going to be a different kind of news. They had easy access to me and knew I would probably answer what I could, but, at that moment, they were friends and not reporters. Their compassion showed. So when Dan asked them to wait a few minutes to let me collect myself, they did.

On their way out, though, one of them asked for a picture of Rich so they could at least start their stories. I glanced at the only clean corner of my desk and looked into Rich's gorgeous blue eyes. He was in his U.N. uniform, a version of the Marine field uniform with a U.N. patch on one sleeve and an American flag on the other. His light blue beret covered the balding scalp of which he was embarrassed and matched his eyes perfectly. He was posing in a relaxed position on some rocks. There was just a hint of a smile on his lips — the same kind of smile he'd give me when we were in the middle of a really satisfying conversation.

The ticking of the clock grew louder again. I watched myself stare at the picture and was only faintly surprised as it changed in my mind into a picture of Rich and me, together that last weekend in Jerusalem, when we talked about the dangers of his position.

Oh, Rich. Where are you? This can't be true. Maybe they're all mistaken, I heard myself think.

Another part of me knew that it was true. Everything Rich and I had ever done, the talks we'd had, and the love we'd shared had all been events which led to this point in time. There was so much to think about that I didn't even know where to begin. Of course, I'd have to tell Chrissy. Of course, I'd have to be strong. Of course, I wanted to cry. Above all, I wanted to be with Rich, to offer comfort, to help, to make everything better. I couldn't do it all. But then an amazing thing happened.

I had some form of out-of-body experience. My consciousness was transported to Lebanon for a moment. I could see what I was doing, and I could hear what I was thinking. A part of me was shouting, this can't be happening! Another part of me said more gently, we knew this could happen. It's real. Deal with it.

The center of my chest became so terribly heavy that I just knew my heart was going to burst out, falling to the floor in thousands of pieces. But as I was floating, I saw my uniform and remembered that I was a Marine. I had a duty to perform, just like Rich did. I knew I must remember that. I needed to act with composure. I needed to do it the way Rich would have done.

The ticking grew fainter, and the air seemed to sharpen. I took a deep breath. And then I saw him. I don't know where we were, some nameless, spaceless place where our hearts and souls melded.

My heart cried, and my soul apologized. I offered him all the strength I possessed; I knew he would need it. But he offered me his instead. He knew this situation would be hard for all of us. I tried to explain that it was my fault, that if I had been thinking about him before the kidnapping occurred, he would have been safe. I so dearly wanted him to be safe.

I'll do everything I can, Rich, I said as we held each other. I'll get everything under control and work around the clock.

He looked into my eyes and touched my soul once again. Robin, he said, you need to keep yourself well and take care of Chrissy. We'll work this out.

Then with no further words, I apologized from a place in my spirit I didn't even know existed. I wanted him to know that I believed it was still my fault, that I accepted total responsibility for his abduction. If I'd only been thinking about him when he was taken, I could have made him think of me at the same time, and the whole thing never would have happened. He would have been more careful then. Or maybe if we'd had that instant of closeness that we shared so easily when we were physically together, he'd have traveled a different route.

My anguish cried out to him. Because I'd let him down, I needed to assume responsibility for rectifying the situation. His soul hushed mine. His heart said he was okay. He reminded me that we could work together to get him out.

Then the spacelessness evaporated. I was back at my desk. I'd only been in my cubbyhole for three minutes since first hearing the news. But I knew now what I had to do. My Marine training returned, as I knew Rich wanted it to, and I looked again at his picture. I whispered to him, I'll be strong, Rich. This won't be a problem. We'll win. I know my mission. It's to protect you and get you home, but right now, it's to be a good Marine and Pentagon press officer.

My hand quivering, but my mind resolute, I handed the photo to Bill Harlow to give to the reporters.

Captain Rich Higgins, infantry battalion advisor to the
Vietnamese Marine Corps, Republic of Vietnam, 1972

Robin Lee Ross,
State University of New York
At Oneonta, 1972

Chapter 3

Once a Marine...

The acrid belch of a mortar propelled a hissing parachute flare high into the night sky over the Marine headquarters near Monkey Mountain, south of DaNang Air Base. Five hundred yards in the air, the flare ignited with a crack and flooded the perimeter with a steely white light. In the distance, shadows danced. Were they North Vietnamese 122-mm. rocket squads, trying out their new weapons from Russia? Vietnamese Army patrols, assisting their U.S. Marine comrades? Foolhardy Vietnamese civilians making their way home after a long, hard night digging tunnels for the Viet Cong? Second Lieutenant Rich Higgins knew one thing for sure. Whoever they were, he'd sure as hell be sleeping better tonight if he were back home in Louisville, Kentucky. But here in Vietnam was where he was needed, and here he'd stay till his tour was up.

As Rich grew up and the family moved from Lancaster to Covington then finally to Louisville, Kentucky, there was something that kept him whole and that quickly separated him from all the other boys: He heard the calling. As far back as he could remember, he dreamed of becoming a Marine.

He was born William Richard Higgins in Danville, Kentucky, on January 15, 1945, to William and Ethel Higgins. Called by his middle name to distinguish him from his daddy, who was called Billy, Rich fit well into life in the small Louisville suburb of Okalona. He went to church with his family, participated in their youth group, respected others, did well in school, and, like many local boys, he loved cars. When he was a student at Southern High School in Louisville, Rich played for the high school football team. While his talent as an athlete may have been questioned, nobody could doubt his guts and determination.

During the school year when he wasn't on the field for a game or practice, Rich cruised around town with his friends. They'd stop for an A&W and then move on to White Castle for a bag of burgers. But for Rich, there was more to life than just coasting along the easiest path. While his friends spent their summers lazily cruising the strip or fishing and telling lies, Rich held down a series of tough jobs, working long hours tirelessly and cheerfully, always with a goal. He wanted to chart his own course.

His leadership and teaching abilities were clear even in those early days. Rich could conquer any challenge. He learned how to adjust the carburetor in his car's engine so it would sound tough. Then he taught all his buddies to do the same. Even in those early days when the boy didn't have much to teach, it was clear that he was destined to lead instead of follow. If Rich had the skills to do something and someone else didn't, he'd show them how. He even taught one friend to knit. Rich wasn't worried about whether he was "cool" or "uncool." Sometimes he'd go to the home of a neighborhood kid and make candy with the friend's mother and daughter.

He graduated from high school in 1963, where he was not only a four-year letterman in football, but also worked on the newspaper and acted in a play or two. He then went on to attend Miami University in

Oxford, Ohio, on a Navy ROTC scholarship. Before college began, he spent two months training in the Mediterranean on the USS INTREPID as part of his Navy ROTC duties. At Miami, Rich joined the drill team during his first year of school. According to his instructor, Lieutenant Colonel Ray J. O'Leary, Rich always "gave it his all." In 1964, he helped O'Leary and the rest of the team take third place at the largest drill meet they'd ever attended.

Clearly, the amorphous freedom that most students look for in college life was not what Rich sought. Neither were the anti-war demonstrations staged by thousands of students in the 1960s. Instead, he pursued his dream with utter determination and focus. Phillip Shriver, the president of Miami University when Rich was there, said, "It was not always easy to wear the uniform in those days, but Rich always wore it with pride: pride in the Corps and pride in his country." During his time in college, the majority of his activities involved Navy ROTC and the realization of his goal. He learned to fly at Corpus Christi in 1965 and earned his parachutist's wings after three weeks of Airborne School.

In 1967, Rich completed his studies at Miami University, received his bachelor's degree, and was rewarded for his work in Navy ROTC. He received the Marine Corps Association Award for excellence in leadership and was commissioned a second lieutenant in the Marine Corps.

Education was important to Rich because it was a way to prove that he wasn't just an easy-going jock and to reassure himself of his own intelligence. He wouldn't be satisfied holding only a bachelor's degree, so during his service, he also earned two master's degrees. The first was in Human Resource Management from Pepperdine University; the second, in political science, was from Auburn University. Ultimately, though, it wasn't his education that gave him the most satisfaction. His chief joy came from being a Marine.

His first assignment was platoon commander of 3rd Platoon, Company C, 1st Battalion, 3rd Marines in Vietnam. His arrival in DaNang was an eye-opening experience. To Rich, the bitterly cold winter nights spent in Quantico, Virginia, training had always been the most miserable weather imaginable. Vietnam taught him otherwise. In Southeast Asia, the sweltering heat, humidity, and incessant swarms of insects made the soldier's life grueling.

Shortly after arriving in that country, Rich was assigned to lead the platoon in mine-clearing operations within the Iron Triangle south of Con Thien. Clearing land mines was a tough and dangerous assignment. Rich's men were rarely in the same place for more than a day at a time, so they constantly had to set up and guard new perimeters. Some companies had the relative luxury of remaining in one place for a while, which allowed them to come to grips with the environment and create a spirit of camaraderie. It was much more difficult for the Marines of Company C, who were constantly on the move.

The roar of the diesel equipment endlessly assaulted their ears. Sniper fire was a perpetual companion. Every night, harassment fire broke out all around the perimeter. The gunfire, constant relocation, and 24-hour watches took their toll on the troops and made a very weary group of young men. It could be seen in their faces. They were tired and stretched to their limit. It was the dry season, and they never had enough water to bathe. The battle dress of fatigues, flack jacket, helmet, weapon, and other gear added as much as a third more to each man's body weight. Sweat crusted their bodies, and each man's clothing slowly rotted off in the heat and dirt. At night they would dig and dig again until the foxholes met their company's requirements for depth and field of fire. Then they would "stand to" for the hour that it took for the sun to set and darkness to fall.

Mike McClung was one of the men who knew Rich well. At the time, Mike was also a second lieutenant and commanded Charlie Company's 2nd platoon. "Rich and I would take the midnight-to-morning watch for our command posts and meet at the edge of our respective areas each night," Mike wrote. "There we would share coffee and talk. Rich liked to talk about tactics and ways to improve our ability to take the battle to the enemy. Sometimes we rehashed old encounters to see where we could improve. Then we would slip quietly from foxhole to foxhole along the perimeter and talk to our men. Sometimes we shared coffee; other times we would listen to the young Marines talk about home or their fears. But each night, we kept the circle going endlessly — never letting the men fall asleep, always watching and bolstering."

During one of the area sweeps, Charlie Company re-entered a village they had tackled before — the same village where a platoon member had lost a leg earlier in a mine explosion. No one looked forward to the assignment. Rich and his men followed standard operating procedures. Once inside a known minefield, the troops would shift from a squad-spread formation to fire teams in single file. This reduced to one the number of entrances into the minefield and decreased the odds of inadvertently stepping on a mine. Only moments into the field, two Marines were wounded by a booby-trapped hand grenade they'd missed on their sweep. While neither man's injury was life-threatening, the explosion did nothing to settle the nerves of the anxious troops.

Later during the operation, a deafening explosion sounded. A body flew through the air. Amid the chaos and screaming that followed, Rich made his way to the wounded Marine, who lay in the six-foot pit left by the detonated mine. The screaming soldier, split open from groin to chest, clearly would not live long. Rich knelt beside him, watching the life ebb from his internal organs. He held the man's head and shoulders in a comforting embrace and started talking. He told the dying man that the medevac helicopter was coming, reassuring him that help was on the way. The Marine died in Rich's arms three minutes later.

Later in the evening, when the operations were complete and the perimeter secured, Rich was much quieter than usual. His troops understood. He was grieving over the loss of one of his Marines.

On December 16, 1967, the 3rd Platoon, with Lieutenant Higgins at its helm, had been ordered to sweep and secure the first in a group of bunker complexes along the South China Sea about 4,000 meters south of the Demilitarized Zone. The compound consisted of a series of rectangular wooden bunkers covered with sand and topped with sandbags. Eight-foot-high sand dunes connected the bunkers and formed the structure. The entrance to the compound faced the sea and had a natural moat of waist-high water. To the east was more sea; to the south a rice paddy created a free-fire zone; to the west were more dunes; and to the north was a vast flat area, another free-fire zone, beyond which lay a line of trees. Unbeknownst to the men of 3rd Platoon, the North Vietnamese Army (NVA) had found an old school building and set up operations in that line of trees. As the Americans came through, they had their first major encounter with the NVA.

Fierce fighting ensued. Although Rich's men eventually succeeded in driving the NVA back, there were several casualties. Rich had called in air support for assistance, but the planes fired too close. Some of his troops were burned by napalm from one of the jets. Once again, Rich grieved for his Marines.

About a month later, another platoon — the 2nd — from Company C was out on a routine patrol of the area's perimeter. Rich's platoon was at his patrol base camp, and the 1st Platoon had headed north, in a fire line, to conduct another sweep of what was now familiar territory. As the 2nd Platoon entered the flat area, they were ambushed.

The NVA had run communication wire through the area and had also built several small covered holes, called spider traps, where lone soldiers could rise from the holes, fire, and then disappear underground for protection. When the platoon was well within the center of the ambushers' kill zone, the NVA opened up with automatic weapons fire. Some Marines were hit; others scrambled to rescue their brethren.

Rich, who was at camp, heard what was happening on the radio. He gathered his men, informed them of the ambush, and called on the radio for situation reports from the platoons. Although he wanted to lend immediate assistance to the fallen Marines, it was essential that he contact the platoon on perimeter patrol so that they could notify Rich of the severity of the situation. When both platoons were rejoined, he gave the order to saddle up. All the while he knew that the only chance of survival for the Americans lay in breaking up the ambush.

Rich knew that the NVA was probably deployed in the shape of a "U," leaving no exit for the ensnared platoon. Rich also knew that he'd need to take out one side of the trap in order to rescue the men. Because he had a good idea of the formation of the NVA ambush, Rich was able to make sound decisions and maneuver his men safely through the heavy enemy mortar fire. He planned an assault through a bunker complex on one side of the trap.

Mounted on two M-48 tanks, Rich and his platoon charged out of the complex and went full throttle up the beach to the north. His Marines hung on to the tank for dear life with one hand and clutched their automatic weapons with the other. Their goal was to follow Lieutenant Higgins into the thick of it in order to save their fellow Marines.

With the help of the M-48s and Rich's insight into the formation of the ambush, the two platoons systematically eliminated the attackers on one side. During this counterattack, Rich remained in the front. He worked side-by-side with the troops to eliminate the pockets of enemy fire, and he joined others to pull the wounded from the battlefield.

Charlie Company emerged victorious. Afterward, Rich personally visited each of his men to thank them and make sure they were all right. He found that he had lost another man in the fight. Stung by the loss, he redoubled his efforts to keep them safe.

Rich's action during the ambush made him a hero, and he was awarded the Bronze Star. He was called a "pit bull on the battlefield," and a man of "real steel." More importantly to Rich, though, he was admired by his men. They looked to him for guidance and support, confident that if they were in trouble he would help them. As Corporal Lee Levesque said, "Lieutenant Higgins was our platoon leader by directive of the Corps. To all the grunts in the our platoon — 'the third herd' — he was just another grunt who shared the same uniform, sweated as hard as we did, agonized over the loss of a brother Marine, and enjoyed telling and listening to tales of family and home. He placed God first, his fellow Marines second, and himself third. Heroic action on his part or that of any of his men was looked upon as the norm, and no awards were expected. Helping one Marine in need on the battlefield was only a small token of gratitude for his having helped you."

For every time that Rich was glorified by his work, he was humbled by the incomprehensible ways in which Marines were slain on the battlefield. Even if it were not his own man, he still felt the loss for the Corps and for the man's family. Rich knew it was the ultimate sacrifice, giving one's life with the hope that a greater good would come from the tragedy of war. Other soldiers knew the respect Rich had for his troops. Mike McClung, platoon commander of 2nd Platoon in Company C, once conducted a search with Rich for a wounded Marine who was hiding from the enemy. McClung remembered, "We finally found him, but we were too late. Although we had all adopted a stoic shell, I knew Rich wanted as badly as I did to find that kid alive. For Rich, the most important part of the Marine Corps was the young men that made up the Corps, and he would do almost anything for any Marine."

Lieutenant Higgins' attitude made a strong impression on Lance Corporal Steve Brown, who served with Rich in Vietnam in 1968. As a fire team leader in the third squad of the 3rd Platoon of Rich's troops, Brown — who served as pack mule for an M-60 machine gun, carried an M-79 grenade launcher, walked the point, and ferreted NVA soldiers from their tunnels — was in a good position to measure the mettle of his platoon leader. "Lieutenant Higgins was 22, and I was all of 18," Corporal Brown recalled. "He was a grunt's officer. He always put his men first. I don't think he slept at night. He would go from foxhole to foxhole to check on us, to see how we were doing or to just talk about the fear of dying."

In Vietnam, Rich's men so admired him that an amateur artist in the platoon drew up a banner with the motto, "Higgins' Heroes," and a picture of Lieutenant Higgins charging into the battle with his platoon following behind.

Rich finished his first tour in Vietnam and returned stateside in 1969. Once back home, he served at Marine Corps Headquarters and then, in 1970, served as the officer-in-charge of the Officer Selection team in Louisville, Kentucky. But Rich missed being in action. He always sought the opportunity to get back into the fight and to command troops.

In 1972, Captain Rich Higgins returned to Vietnam for a second tour. This time he served as infantry battalion advisor to the Vietnamese Marine Corps and later as rifle company commander. As with his first tour, it wasn't long before Rich had established a reputation as a dedicated, highly principled soldier who lived to serve his God, his country, and his Corps. After his second Vietnam tour was over, he returned to the East Coast where he served in Washington and at Quantico, Virginia, until 1977, when he was promoted to major and transferred to Camp Lejeune, North Carolina.

While in North Carolina, again leading Marines in the field, Rich jumped at the opportunity to attend Air Force Command and Staff College, eager to improve his academic and leadership skills. In 1980, he graduated with distinction and was assigned to serve at Marine Corps Headquarters in Washington, D.C. It was there that he was selected to work at the Pentagon in the Office of the Secretary of Defense where he was to serve in a variety of jobs, ultimately as the junior military assistant to Secretary of Defense Caspar Weinberger.

The Pentagon post required a military professional of Rich's caliber — someone with a solid academic background and impeccable judgment and instincts combined with proven initiative. In addition, Secretary Weinberger wanted someone who could command the respect of and deal effectively with influential people. While at the Pentagon, Rich worked closely with Army Major General Colin Powell, then the senior military assistant to Weinberger.

Rich remained at the Pentagon for almost seven years before acting again on his instinct to lead in the field. He quietly applied for an assignment with the United Nations Truce Supervision Organization (UNTSO) and was eventually offered the prestigious and politically delicate command position. When Rich told Secretary Weinberger and Major General Powell that he had been offered the job and would like to leave to take it, they expressed their regret and voiced their concerns about his safety. However, neither wanted to stand in the way of Rich's military career.

The UNTSO position gave him an excellent opportunity to further hone his leadership skills. Prior to this assignment, Rich had commanded only U.S. forces. In his new capacity, he would be in charge of soldiers from seventeen different countries. It was a hard, dangerous job, but as always, Rich relished the challenge. Within just a few months, he would find out how dangerous it really was.

☆☆☆☆☆

Rich, Robin and Chrissy Higgins
Receive a farewell handshake from
Secretary of Defense Caspar W.
Weinberger, The Pentagon, June 1987

Robin is promoted to captain,
Washington, DC, 1980

Rich and Robin Higgins,
wedding day,
Jacksonville, North Carolina, December 23, 1977

Chapter 4

A Nice Jewish Girl
From Long Island

Quantico, Virginia
1976

Robin Ross become a Marine officer? Hah! At least that's what I would have said while I was in college and still single. Growing up, I never imagined myself choosing the military. After all, I was from a family of academics and didn't know anything about military life. If anything, I was "a-military," in the way that amoebas are asexual. I didn't even meet my first Marine until I was a year out of college. What a turnaround that day was.

I was born in 1950 in the Bronx, New York, and lived on Long Island until I left for college. My father, Dr. Norman Ross, was a high school English teacher who taught me early in life to appreciate the power of language. The first-born of Norman and Thelma Ross, my parents always made me feel destined for something special. I think that's part of being the first-born child in a Jewish family — there are high hopes for all the children, but there are grandiose dreams for the life of the first child. After all, when our parents are gone, we are the ones responsible for keeping the family together, passing down stories, and preserving our heritage. Even though my parents loved all four of their kids with the same passionate intensity, they expected more from me because I was the oldest.

Like many first-born Jewish kids of my generation, by the time my family settled down in our suburban Long Island neighborhood, I was too old to begin Hebrew school. I watched my brothers and sister go through the Bar and Bat Mitzvah coming-of-age rites. Although the ceremonies were intriguing, I didn't feel I had really missed anything. I was Jewish, of course, but for me it had more do to with morals and ideas than religious rituals.

In high school, I began to realize how important Jewish values were to me. I wrote a report on Mordecai Kaplan and became fascinated by his work. Kaplan stressed the concepts of Jewish civilization and peoplehood, ideas with which I identified strongly. He understood that our times were vastly different from those of the Hebrew Bible and that gender equality was far more important today than in the past. He focused on converting the Talmud and Jewish laws into ethical concepts that were relevant to contemporary society. Kaplan emphasized the importance of recognizing all people as equal under God. His ideas captivated me because they were rooted in cultural heritage and diversity rather than theological dogma.

Kaplan put into words the thoughts and feelings I had struggled with for years. I could never understand the hatred human beings could have toward others. How could people, especially those who were vocal about religious ethics, have so much animosity toward others simply because they had different appearances or beliefs? While searching for my own identity, I'd lie in my room for hours asking "Why?" and "How?" and "What can I do?" Reading Kaplan helped me put my rhetorical and philosophical questions into perspective. He made me think about how living a Jewish life might help me answer them.

His writings provided a real-world context for a scholarly exploration of my Jewish heritage. I could read all that I wanted to satisfy my academic cravings. At the same time, though, I could practice the idea of being Jewish as he conceived it. It didn't matter that I wasn't a Bat Mitzvah, didn't know Hebrew, and wasn't schooled in the Talmud.

I could be Jewish on my own terms. Although I didn't know it then, this ability to define my Jewishness would later stand me in very good stead.

When I finished high school, I attended the State University of New York (SUNY) at Oneonta. I'd never lived beyond Long Island and had been really quite comfortable in my cocoon. College life changed all that.

It was the late 1960s. The entire country was in turmoil. There were student riots across the country over a war that many people of my generation felt was wrong. It seemed like everyone was involved in some aspect of the Vietnam conflict. It was easy to get caught up in the action even if you didn't really understand all the issues.

Some of it was even fun. There were sleep-outs in the campus quadrangle, and occasionally classes were boycotted as a part of the protest. Once, a few SUNY students pushed the limit by trying to take down the American flag, but others eventually talked them out of it.

Yet, when the anti-war movement really started to take off, I was confused. I'd never been interested in the military and still didn't really know much about what was going on in the world around me. On the television and in the papers, they called the fighting in Vietnam a "conflict," as if it was an argument that could be easily resolved. But on campus, students called it a "war." They said innocent people were being killed, including boys of our age — boys who should have and could have been in school with us. I heard that a boy I had gone to high school with had been killed in Vietnam, but I hadn't known him well.

I didn't know enough about Vietnam to crusade against it. At the same time, I didn't want to be left out of something that so clearly was impacting America. Rather than join the movement for the mere sake of joining, or dropping out of school to return to the safety of home, I made a bold move. I decided to go to Israel for my junior year in 1970.

It was a daring decision for me. Traveling alone halfway across the world was frightening for a girl who had always been a bit of a loner. I wasn't really sure why I wanted to go to Israel, what I would find there, or whether or not I would like it, but I needed to find out what was beyond my isolated New York horizons. I needed to see past my inhibitions and take control of my fears. When I got to Israel, I learned to do just that.

The trip was a turning point in my life. I arrived in Israel in August of 1970 in the middle of the incredibly dry, fly-and-scorpion-filled desert near Kibbutz Sde Boker, home of Israel's first Prime Minister, David Ben-Gurion. Since all the students were Americans, there to learn about the country, we were given a Hebrew test right away. Because I didn't know even one word of the language, I ended up in what we affectionately called the tipsha class — the class for "the stupid ones."

Luckily, I met Reuven Gordon there. His real name was Bob, but we were, after all, in Israel, so his Hebrew name stuck. Reuven was tall and dark. His olive skin and sunken, brown eyes were intensely Semitic-looking. His disheveled clothes and constantly tousled, curly brown hair made him always look as if he just woke up. But I think I fell for him as I fell for the country we were in. It was all so magical.

Reuven eased some of the trepidation I had about being so far from home, because he was also from New York. Through him, I made new friends: Mina, Jeff, Ya'el, and Meir. With this group of compatriots, I learned about myself and my Jewishness. I also learned about the true nature of the world around me for the first time.

My friends and I toured every place we could in Reuven's Land Rover. One day we went up to Masada, a remote hilltop fortress, and climbed the winding path just before dawn. Towering far above the Judean Desert, Masada is a symbol of courage and love of freedom. For three years, Roman Legions laid siege to the 960 Jewish men, women, and children who had taken refuge there. On Passover in 73 C.E., the Jewish zealots, acknowledging their cause was lost, committed mass suicide rather than fall under the yoke of Roman slavery.

Our only guides were flashlights, but we made it to the top just before sunrise. Then, when the sun rose over the peaks of Jordan, we looked down at the Dead Sea and imagined the Romans looking back at us. Some of the kids smoked hashish to make the experience seem more mystical, but I didn't need it. It was such a glorious view by itself that I floated anyway and wondered if God saw the world this way all the time.

Another time we went deep into the Negev Desert to see a meteor shower. We found a perfect spot to spread out an old blanket to lie on. I'd never been anyplace that was so dark in my whole life. I'm sure I could see every single star that existed. Then, as we were lying there, the meteor shower started. Thousands of stars were tumbling out of the sky. It was beautiful and cosmic. On the way home, I remembered where we were and what the world was really like.

Israel was a land of paradox. The terrain was gorgeous, the desert was intriguing, and the people were amazing. My friends and I eventually shared an apartment in a suburb of Jerusalem, and occasionally we'd go into the Old City. We'd walk along narrow, noisy streets and listen to the vendors hawk their goods from little pushcarts or cramped stalls. Sheepskin coats, vests, and slippers hung everywhere. The scent of teas from the cafes and the hashish smoked in crooked alleyways contrasted with the ubiquitous donkey dung and the sewage that streamed by in open rivulets.

Israel was also a land of war. At dawn on the way home from the Negev Desert after the meteor shower, we saw signs cautioning us to beware of the minefields. And when Ya'el brought me to meet her family who lived on Kibbutz Dafna near the border, I was stunned at the sight of all the Israelis my age, hitchhiking along the side of the roads with their guns slung over their shoulders. They carried them as casually as I would carry my backpack. The army was an omnipresent fact of Israeli life, but one that was totally foreign to me. Long before we in the U.S. would become used to having our bags searched before entering government buildings, Israelis accepted this as a part of everyday life.

However, after a few months in Israel I began to understand more about Jewish life and culture. Judaism stressed ethics and the importance of community. That's why there are so many *kibbutzim* and *moshavim* (collective and communal farms). That's also why mandatory military service seems natural to Israelis. All Jews are expected to work for the good of their community. In a beautiful book, which I read many years later, called *To Life*, Rabbi Harold Kushner explains it this way: "We are called on to do something for God and for the world. We are important; and we are empowered. It is our obligation to be a role model for all nations."

By March, Israel felt like home. My life seemed complete. I'd play *shesh-besh* (backgammon) with Israelis, and we'd muddle along, trying to understand one another's language. I'd walk for miles up the hills at Ein Kerim just to be among the olive trees, waving at people I didn't know. I fit in with Israel and all its contradictions, and I wondered if I'd ever actually lived before arriving there.

I left Israel in May 1971 with mixed feelings. I was glad to be seeing my family again, but there was a sense of leaving a piece of me behind, a piece I'd worked hard to find. Once again Kushner's writing summed up my feelings: "Judaism is less about believing and more about belonging. It is less about God and more about what we owe each other, because we believe God cares more about how we treat each other than he does about our theology." I vowed I'd return, for it was in Israel that I'd truly found my soul.

Back in New York, I was restless. I knew I no longer belonged there, but I also knew that I had to finish college and get my degree. That was also part of my heritage.

I floated through my last semester at college in Oneonta. I got a fish tank and a waterbed and became involved in Transcendental Meditation. In this fluid state, good grades came easily. I earned my bachelor's degree in English and maintained a perfect 4.0 grade point average the last semester.

Eventually my boyfriend Reuven and I drifted apart, and although we kept in touch from time to time, I was deeply saddened to hear he died young some years later.

While my friends were applying for positions with New York elementary schools, I wrote to exotic places overseas. I watched my friends start their teaching careers, and soon realized no one overseas was going to beg me to come to work for them. My former classmates all found themselves teaching fourth grade; I found myself behind the counter of Sholkoff's Opticians, selling eyeglasses. I was bored out of my mind, so I went back to school, my tail between my legs, and worked on earning a master's degree and a teaching certificate. My dad was a teacher, as were my cousins and my friends. I naturally felt that I, too, was destined to become one.

During graduate school, I got valuable practical experience in student teaching. My life seemed to be back on track, and I felt I could conquer the world — or at least the demons that lived in the hearts and minds of America's 16-year-olds. I would inspire them to lofty heights and develop in them love and respect for themselves and others. I began applying for positions in nearby high schools. After my interviews, I would return home, anxiously awaiting a phone call that never came. Whenever I passed a high school, my heart sank. I started substitute teaching just for the practice and began to wonder if I really wanted to teach. I went to San Francisco and worked as a switchboard operator for a short time. Then I came back, applied, interviewed, and substituted some more.

I started to worry that I might never find a real teaching job, so I began to look at my alternatives. I wanted to use my degree and end up a professional who was respected for the job she did. I wanted responsibility and needed to be challenged. That's when my father suggested the military.

My friends thought I was crazy. They asked me if I really wanted to cut my hair and wear stockings every day. In my own mind, I was convinced that the military was just what I needed. I took the Navy officer candidate application test and failed. There was too much physics and math for me, an English major. Then the unexpected happened: I received a letter from a high school that wanted me! It seemed my luck had finally changed. I was going to be a teacher after all.

I taught for a year. The kids were great, but school wasn't what I thought it would be. It seemed more like a factory than a place of learning. The head of the English Department told me not to teach Shakespeare or grammar because it would "turn the kids off." How, I wondered, do you teach English without teaching those subjects?

My colleagues were fine, but they went through the motions day after day, without ever looking to the future, questioning the present, or reflecting on the past. I hated the job. There was no respect, no discipline, and no organization. Neither the students nor the teachers had the ability to look beyond the world of the small school and see that there was more out there. The future held so much potential, but no one realized it. The sense of community that I had grown to love in Israel was conspicuously absent here. Maybe that was because our country was still so torn apart over the Vietnam War.

My negative experience at the high school raised new questions. I knew there was something out there more fulfilling for me. My father had raised me to believe I was special, and I knew there was a higher calling for my life. It didn't take me very long to realize that it wasn't teaching high school.

Luckily for the students and for me, I was laid off after my first year. Right away I went back down to the Navy recruiting office. Once again, I failed their test, which made it easier to realize that I didn't particularly want to join that branch anyway. So I went to the Air Force, but their officer course was closed. They told me I could enlist and work my way up, perhaps, but by then I was on fire. I didn't want to settle for the bottom rung of the ladder, even though I knew I could work my way up. I left the Air Force office and thought about the Army, but the training films they had me watch, the overwhelming size of that force, and the "Today's Army" ads didn't appeal to me. I stood in the unemployment line for two weeks before I finally screwed up my courage to talk to the Marine recruiters.

As soon as I walked into the Marine recruiting office, I knew I was in the right place. My doubts began to wane. They looked and acted sharp. They were intelligent and sensitive. I filled out their application and took their entrance test. To my amazement and joy, I was soon accepted. When I raised my hand to take the oath as a commissioned officer in the United States Marine Corps, I was convinced that I had made the right choice. Before I knew it, I was on my way to Officers' Candidate School in Quantico, Virginia. What ever had I done!

My first few weeks at women officers' training at Quantico were quite different from what I had expected. All I did was clean, sew, wash, and iron. On good days, I was allowed to do some physical training and basic drills. At The Basic School, the follow-on training all new officers get at Quantico, it didn't get much better. The senior officers there ranted about the importance of responsibility, but gave us none. I thought that if I were a military police officer in the Marines, I'd get the responsibility that I wanted. And, I wanted to get far away from teaching English.

I asked for and received a military police occupational specialty, finished my training, and was assigned back to Quantico, Virginia.

Ironically, I returned to Quantico as an English teacher, not as a cop. My title was Effective Communication Specialist. In this role, though, I was finally given the real duties that I had been craving. I was charged with developing, writing, and teaching a course in effective writing at The Basic School. I was left to my own devices to create and implement something that would work. I commanded no troops, but I was important to each Marine officer that passed through my classroom. I made the decisions. And people — those I taught and those who were over me — liked what I was doing.

I was finally satisfied. I had a direction, and I fit in. I was now a whole person: as a woman, a Jew, and a Marine. The nice little Jewish girl from Long Island was now whole and fulfilled. She had found a home for herself in the Marines.

☆☆☆☆☆

Rich and Robin at their final
Marine Corps Birthday Ball,
Washington, DC
November 10, 1986

Chapter 5

Love, Marine Style

I wasn't all that impressed when I first met Captain Rich Higgins at Quantico. It was the first day of my first tour after returning from military police training. I was a brand-new second lieutenant, still adventurous, and I identified more with the slightly unkempt, burly, long-haired hippies I'd known in Israel and New York than the clean-cut Marine types.

A mutual friend of ours tried to set up a date between Rich and me, but it seemed that neither of us was very much interested. After all, I was a Long Island Jewish girl who liked hippies. Rich was a conservative, Christian Southerner who'd always wanted to be a Marine. What could we possibly have in common?

One night, by chance, we were both at the Officers' Club. It was the Friday of Labor Day weekend, 1976. Rich and I started talking, and as the evening progressed, I was amazed at how comfortable the conversation felt. We went to dinner that night at a restaurant in Quantico, and we both knew right then that we would be together for a long, long time.

I'm still not sure how it happened so quickly, but we knew, in a matter of moments, that this was the real thing. While Rich had always known what he wanted to do and had single-mindedly pursued his goals, I had made painstaking efforts to find myself. As a Marine, I finally knew what I wanted. Perhaps it was this shared confidence that created our first bond.

In any event, it was obvious that Rich and I loved each other deeply. After a few months of intense togetherness, we were even more convinced. I took Rich to meet my family, and he and my grandma hit it off right away. Grandma Shirley took me aside and scolded me gently, "If you lose him, it'll be your fault!" Rich took me home to meet his family as well. His sweet mother allowed me into her kitchen to get her biscuit recipe. Rich's sisters later confided in me that even they never had that honor.

Then fate intervened. I was shipped out to Okinawa, Japan, and Rich was assigned to Camp Lejeune, North Carolina. Some of our friends wondered if our relationship would survive. Rich and I wondered, too. Although neither of us looked forward to our forced separation, we were Marines first. Our commitment to our country and our duties to the Corps were, after all, part of our bond.

In addition, we had individual doubts. Rich had goals for himself. He was single-minded in his vision of leading troops once again in the field. He wasn't sure love and a new wife were part of this dream. Anyway, he had just come out of a painful divorce and didn't want to let his guard down. I had just embarked on an exciting career and was finally discovering qualities in me that made me proud to be a Marine officer. Did I want to give that up for someone else's dreams?

We wrote each other daily. When we found that unsatisfactory, we would call. We talked often, and quickly ran up enormous phone bills. There was so much to share. I wanted to know how he was doing and what was going on in his world. He was just as interested in mine. We weren't merely lovers; we were best friends and the closest of confidantes.

I thought if our long distance relationship survived MARS, the Military Affiliate Radio System, we could endure anything. When our phone budgets had been stretched to their limits, we used this military ham radio system to communicate. We could still hear each other's voice, but it took incredible patience. After each transmission, we had to say "Over," then wait, and finally receive a response that was also followed by "Over." Even though the distance made it difficult, we kept at it. We had to. Rich and I knew that something special was happening, and we had decided to let it. And we had the discipline to stick with it.

Sometimes we'd send messages to one another through Marines who traveled between Okinawa and Camp Lejeune. This was our favorite way of staying in touch. The people who came and went didn't always do so on a set schedule, but at least when they carried our letters and little gifts for each other, we knew they would arrive safely. Marines are taught to put the Corps first. If a fellow officer needed something done, even a seemingly trivial task like carrying a love letter, it would be done.

Our relationship continued through correspondence the entire time we were separated. All the while, our love grew stronger. Sometimes I felt as if my heart knew what his was feeling every moment of every day. Our connection was so close that it scared me sometimes. One day in September of 1977, Rich and I were both writing. He was writing a letter to my grandmother, and I was writing a poem to him. Rich wrote to my grandmother,

> *Robin and I write often because we love each other very much. Absence has made the heart grow fonder and also allowed the mind to decide with whom I would like to spend the rest of my life... We have shared an awful lot of emotions together and are very compatible. Plus, Grandma, she is just a wonderful person and I love her and am happy with her. Just between you and me we both grew up an awful lot last year, we both needed to, for different reasons, but we needed to and we did it together. Grandma, I have decided to ask Robin to be my wife. I haven't told her yet, but I'm sure she feels it.*

In my poem to Rich, I was expressing my uncertainty about the future, my need for answers, and my enduring faith in him. I wrote,

> *Who am I, this child of the sun;*
> *And where shall I go?*
> *Am I to go alone or,*
> *If not, with whom shall I walk*
> *All the days of my life?...*
> *Two frightened and humble fellows*

Armed together, complementing,
The first of a few
A loved and cherished gem in the rough.
And together we grew and
Began to shine, with age, not polish
But knew warmth and love
And oh so many happy days."

To this day, it still surprises me how often Rich and I did this. We were separated by thousands of miles and half a world, but were still thinking the same thoughts at the same time. How fortunate I felt to have found this man.

We talked about marriage without ever saying the word. We knew that after my one-year tour in Okinawa, unless we were married, the Marine Corps could send me anywhere. Then our separation could last years, not months. I think we took it for granted that, of course, we'd be married. I just didn't know when it would happen.

On November 10, 1977, I found out. November 10th is special for all Marines, because on that day we celebrate the birthday of our Corps. For Rich, the Corps' birthday was more meaningful than his own and more festive than New Year's Eve. To him, it was a renewal day, a time to recall history and traditions and look forward to the vision of the future. November 10th was a day of optimism and hope. Rich took it seriously, but he had fun with it, too. He'd find a bottle of Wild Turkey and a silver tray. Carefully, so as not to spill any, he'd open the bottle, place it on the tray and invite his senior enlisted Marines or his junior officers to share a drink with him in celebration. He always had a little of the flamboyant in him.

In Okinawa, we also had a party. I had just come off the parade deck and went to join the festivities. There was a huge cake, lots of commotion, and cries of "Happy Birthday!" back and forth in the office spaces of the Provost Marshal where I worked. Someone came in and told me I had a phone call from a Captain Higgins.

I ran to the phone, but before I could even finish "hello," Rich was singing, "Happy Birthday, Marine, will you come home and marry me?" I didn't cry. I would have looked ridiculous standing at a birthday party, dressed in my Marine uniform, with tears streaming down my cheeks. Instead, I had the same absolute contentment that I knew when I lay on the sand watching that meteor shower in the Negev so long ago. I belonged. My soul was complete.

We decided to marry on my birthday, December 23, 1977. Rich promised that he'd make all the arrangements stateside and said all I needed to do was get a dress. I found a wonderful seamstress in Okinawa and had my wedding dress handmade from a picture I found in a magazine. It was very simple, with a little white ribbon and a bit of lace. Rich had the invitations printed and mailed and even sent me one. My dad announced our engagement in the local paper on December 8th, and I asked for my 18-days stateside leave from Okinawa. I arrived in Camp Lejeune a few days before the wedding, and Rich and I were married on my birthday at the Protestant Chapel at seven in the evening.

While I was in Okinawa, Rich had bought us a house. Since I had less than two weeks before I had to return to Okinawa for another six months, we spent our honeymoon at our new home. On the morning after the wedding, there was a knock at our front door. A neighbor had come to invite Rich for Christmas dinner. The quiet, friendly bachelor who had lived there had always seemed a bit lonely to her. She seemed shocked to see a young woman answering the door at this early hour, but after a few minutes we all laughed about it as Rich introduced me as his new wife.

That time was heaven, and Rich and I cemented our commitment to one another as best friends, lovers, and now husband and wife. Even though our backgrounds were vastly different, our separate journeys through life taught us both the importance of belonging and trust. We had deep admiration for one another and shared the same values: not only a love for each other, but also for our community, our country, and the Corps.

Before we were married, we knew what being a Marine couple would entail. Our assignments could create long separations, but for us that was natural. Whenever a new assignment came along, we'd talk about it. Invariably we would decide that accepting the position, no matter where it was, would enhance our careers and our abilities as Marines. As two people who loved each other completely, we also knew that anything that made the other happy, proud, and content would also make us stronger as a couple.

There's an old adage in the Marine Corps. It says that a separation will break apart a bad marriage and make a good marriage stronger. Rich and I truly believed this. We each wanted to be better Marines, for ourselves and for each other. It increased our respect and admiration for each other. We loved the idea of being one of a few married Marine couples and took that role seriously. If we succeeded, it would pave the way for others to live and love in the Marines.

In our first three years of marriage we spent a total of six months together. During the separations we'd talk and write, just as we had during our courtship. Now, we also shared our projects and reports with one another. It was a way to keep up with our separate lives, and both of us enjoyed being editors for each other. This gave us a fresh perspective on what we'd done and helped align the way we thought. We learned how both of our minds worked, and this brought us even closer together.

In 1980, we began to live like a normal family. We moved to Washington, DC, and to a life without separations. Chrissy, Rich's ten-year-old daughter by his previous marriage, came from Germany to live with us. We had all the makings of a settled American family. Rich was working at the Pentagon with Secretary Weinberger; I was right up the hill at Headquarters Marine Corps; and Chrissy was safely ensconced in our suburban Virginia community. Soon I was to get a public affairs assignment at the Pentagon, putting Rich and me in the same building and enabling us to carpool together and spend more time with one another.

Several years later when Rich started to think seriously about a job with the United Nations Truce Supervision Operation in the Middle East, we were both excited. It would be a significant career move for him and the next logical step for him as a Marine. We knew there was danger involved in any tour in the Middle East, but this was Rich's chance to make a difference in the world. For a Marine like Rich, his duty to the Corps and to the country mandated that he seize the opportunity in order to make that difference.

I had just been accepted into a prestigious master's program in communications at Boston University. The Marine Corps would pay for the two-year course of study. I would put that off until Rich returned from the Middle East if he were to get the assignment. That way we could keep Chrissy in high school in Virginia, where she was doing very well. There would be time for me later.

Rich and I had it all. I drew strength from him, and he found some in me. His commitment to the military was the inspiration that helped me understand the power of faith and of belief in something outside myself. Our love was absolute, and we cherished the whole being that was the other. My life was him and his was me.

When the U.N. position was offered to Rich, he never considered turning it down. He left for his one-year tour in July 1987. That Christmas, Chrissy and I took time during her semester break to visit him in Israel. It had been 16 years since I had left Israel as a wide-eyed and wild college student. In Jerusalem, where I still think my whole life began, Rich and I celebrated our tenth wedding anniversary, my birthday, and our love. The three of us spent Christmas together there, which was a moving experience for us all. Imagine being surrounded by so much religious and cultural heritage at such an important time of year! Although the weather was a lot like Washington had been in the winter, it didn't seem dreary to us. We were a family once again, safe and secure in one another's arms.

Before Rich had to return to the field, we took a vacation and toured Syria and Egypt. I needed to see where Rich was spending so much of his time. I wanted to know what life was like, what the countryside looked like, so I could take home a memory of where he was. That way, he wouldn't feel so far away when we returned home. Eventually, the time came to leave. The goodbyes were hard, but we were accustomed to them.

The letters I got from Rich after our visit were brief. He was so busy with his new command that there wasn't much time for writing. One of his first responsibilities as Chief, Observer Group Lebanon, was to address a Board of Inquiry convened to investigate the death of Captain Peter McCarthy, an Australian soldier under Rich's command who was killed by a roadside bomb.

On February 8, 1988, I received a letter from Rich that was longer than usual. Despite his busy schedule, he included in his letter his statement to the Board of Inquiry that outlined what he had done in the short time he'd been there and just how much effort had gone into training his men and minimizing potential risk. It was clear that while he was grieving for one of his men, he redoubled his effort to ensure the safety and the morale of the living. Rich's boundless dedication reminded me how lucky I was to have found him.

A few days later, on Valentine's Day 1988, Rich called, and we talked briefly about our love for each other, for his daughter, and for the work that he found so important.

It was the last time I ever spoke with him.

Chapter 6

Network News

They say your life is not a major catastrophe until Dan
Rather tells the world about it on the CBS Evening
News. Now I know that's true. The night that Rich was
kidnapped, I found myself in a mild trance as I looked
at his photo — the one from my desk — which now
appeared on the television screen in a box over Dan
Rather's shoulder. I heard the television anchorman
say, "Another American has been taken hostage in
Lebanon. Gunmen in the violent southern part of the
country today ambushed and kidnapped a U.S. Marine
officer. Lieutenant Colonel William Higgins was the
leader of a U.N. observer team. He became the ninth
American hostage currently held in Lebanon. No group
claimed responsibility. Our report begins with Pentagon
correspondent David Martin...."

Earlier that day, after recovering from the initial shock of Rich's abduction, I quickly started rearranging my life and priorities. My first concern was to notify Chrissy and our parents before they learned about it on the national news. I wanted the family to know that someone was in charge of the situation, that someone was there to care for them — and that "someone" was me. Next, I started to prepare myself to face the hordes of reporters who soon, I knew, would be seeking answers I didn't have to a myriad of questions.

I couldn't let myself fall apart. I wanted to be strong for many reasons. I knew that Rich's captors would be watching for signs of weakness, and I refused to give them any satisfaction. As a Marine officer and military wife, I also knew that I wanted to be a model for other military wives — women who knew deep in their hearts that there, but for the grace of God, went they.

I knew that the American people would be feeling our pain, for we were one of them. I also knew that the other families of men missing in Lebanon would be watching and listening, as would hundreds of other people whose loved ones had been hostages or POWs in the past.

But there was also another reason to rein in my natural emotions and refuse to express them. As a military press officer, I had often seen public officials react negatively when the wife or widow of a hostage broke down in tears or spilled her guts to the cameras. These actions, I knew, sometimes prompted people with critical information to tone it down — or withhold it — if they thought that the recipient couldn't handle the truth or would run to the press. This gave me one more need to appear calm, professional, and in control: so that the men and women at the highest levels of authority knew that I could be trusted with the worst possible information. These same people, I knew, were the ones who would ultimately be involved in bringing Rich home. I wanted them to know that I was an asset, not a liability.

Wednesday afternoon, I had Chrissy brought to the Pentagon from her high school near our home in Woodbridge, Virginia, so that I could tell her face-to-face what had happened, and comfort her. I also knew that Rich would have wanted us together at that time.

And later at home, I focused on ways to get Rich home. I felt twin reasons for my desire to see him safely back: my love for him and natural desire for his safety, and an irrational sense that I was somehow to blame for not being there with him in Lebanon, by his side, as his wife and fellow Marine. All afternoon I tried to push my fears out of my mind and concentrate on something more productive: a plan to secure Rich's safe return.

I kept waiting for a call from him saying that it was over, that they had just made some horrible mistake by taking him, that he had escaped their grasp. The phone rang constantly, but the one call I was waiting for never came.

By dinner time, the outlines of a plan were emerging in my mind. I knew that I would dedicate all my time to obtaining Rich's safe return. I set as my goal to get as many people as possible to adopt Rich's return as one of their top-priority missions. I felt that many leaders would naturally make his safe return a top priority, since Rich was in Lebanon under orders and in the service of his country and the United Nations. I am glad that I didn't know then what I have since learned.

After all the reporters and their microwave trucks had gone and the phone calls slowed to a trickle, we were alone. Myself, Chrissy, and Commander Bob Prucha. That was Dan Howard's doing. He knew, as adept as I had proven myself normally speaking with the press and the general public, this was not "normally." Bob had immediately volunteered to serve as the buffer between us and the world who now wanted to get to us. Bob and I had worked together and knew each other somewhat, but in the ensuing few days would come to share emotions that no two friends should ever have to. Bob answered all the phone calls, talked to all the reporters, even fed us when we needed food.

I let Chrissy call her own shots. She was seventeen, after all, and a young woman. But she was extremely close to her father, so I had to watch for signs of instability. She was a "champ" — as her father would no doubt say. She was very shy about it and did not want to speak with any press, although I told her I'd arrange it if she wanted to. At first, she didn't even want to speak with any of her friends, but that afternoon when I saw a group of them gather on the front lawn and call to her, I was gratified to see her run to speak with them. Our watchdog Prucha hung in the background to make sure the press didn't bother the hugging group.

Later that night, Bob insisted we try to get some sleep. He assured us he would sleep on the couch and continue watching the door and getting the phone. Chrissy and I went upstairs. We were alone together, but we didn't talk much. Chrissy wanted me to tell her it wouldn't be long, to assure her he'd be all right. I wanted to tell her that — but I couldn't and wouldn't lie to her.

It was late by the time we went to bed. But sleep didn't come, only thoughts of the daddy and husband who should have been there. Rich had been gone on his overseas tour for eight months, but the house felt emptier that night than ever.

☆☆☆

Day 2
February 18, 1988

The next day, Rich's father was dead. I knew the day before that Bill Higgins was in a Louisville hospital gravely ill with advanced heart disease. In fact, after that fateful call to let Chrissy know of her dad's kidnapping, my next call was to be to Mary, Rich's older sister. After their mother had died in 1979, Mary had become the matriarch of the family. She sat for hours with her father in the hospital, and I knew she was probably there when news of her brother's kidnapping came.

Before I could find the phone number for the Audubon Hospital, the phone rang at my desk, and it was Mary. I could tell she had been crying. She blurted out that I had to get in touch with Rich to tell him to come home, that her father had just lapsed into a coma. Rich had come home in September 1987 on emergency leave from the Mideast to see him, during an earlier hospital stay. Bill Higgins didn't die then, but it was good that Rich came. It gave the two men a chance to say the things they needed to say to each other, knowing perhaps then that they'd never see each other again. In my last phone conversation with Rich — had it been only three days earlier? — he reminded me that if his father died, he would not be available to come home.

Through the phone line with Mary, I heard the television set in the background at the hospital room. I knew I had to tell Mary quickly before she heard it on the news. I didn't want to shock her, so I said softly, "Mary, I've been trying to call you. Richard isn't where he's supposed to be."

"What do you mean?" she said in a tremulous voice. "It looks as if he may have been kidnapped," I was finally able to say. There was nothing but a stunned silence on the phone.

She needed someone with her at that moment. Her father lay in a coma only inches from where she was, and her little brother had just been kidnapped by terrorists a world away.

I instructed my sister-in-law, now clearly in shock, to hang on the line. I put her on hold and, on the other line, called her husband, Harold, at work at Hillerich and Bradsby. I quickly and frankly told him what was going on, and told him he needed to get to the hospital quickly. Then I punched the blinking button and told Mary that Harold was on his way and that I'd be in touch soon.

The next morning, Bill Higgins, 72, died. He never knew that his only son had been kidnapped.

The Thursday newspapers and television reports were now filled with speculation about Rich's abduction. Lebanese eyewitnesses allegedly stated that he was thrown in the trunk of a red, white, or brown Mercedes or Volvo by two or three men armed with Kalishnikov assault rifles. Someone speculated that a car had passed him and cut him off. Another thought Rich had been flagged down and stopped for someone he recognized or appeared to need help. Neither of these scenarios made any sense to me. Rich had been through defensive driving school in Virginia and had passed with flying colors. Had he been confronted by armed men, he would have sought to avoid or evade them. He wouldn't have stopped, and if they had fired, there would have been bullet damage to the car. There was none.

Another theory was that his radio hadn't worked, and that perhaps it had been tampered with during his meeting with Abdel Majeed Saleh.

This suggestion also made no sense to me. Rich was compulsive about radio checks and other security measures. He would never have departed in a vehicle without having performed all the standard radio checks. Rich was nothing if not thorough.

A newspaper story suggested that the kidnappers drove a series of different cars that couldn't be traced. Private radio stations in Lebanon said that the kidnappers took him to a Palestinian refugee center near Tyre, where they allegedly moved him from a Volvo to a Mercedes Benz and drove away. Others speculated that to avoid Amal militia checkpoints, the kidnappers forded the Litani River and got away. I found myself groping for answers, but there were none. No investigation had yet begun. There were only questions, reactions, speculation, and a great deal of political posturing.

The White House immediately called for Rich's prompt release. A Pentagon official said that President Ronald Reagan was "mad as hell" about the kidnapping, but added that the government would not compound Colonel Higgins' plight by pleading publicly for his release with his captors. "Just as we don't discuss the other hostages, we're not going to discuss Colonel Higgins," he said.

During a photo session with congressional leaders, President Reagan said, "We're doing everything we can... We're trying to get him located, and certainly we want to rescue him." The President's staff quickly downplayed his statement, emphasizing that no military rescue operation was planned. Not that it mattered, for once a hostage disappears into the terrorist bowels of Beirut or the Bekaa Valley, rescue becomes almost impossible. The reason is simple: If you don't know where the person is being held, you can't swarm in and grab him.

Amal chief Nabih Berri, who had met Rich several times, went into a closed session with his military advisors on the night of the kidnapping. His spokesman said that "Amal will not leave a stone unturned in looking for and uncovering the perpetrators."

In Naqoura, Timor Goksell, spokesman for the U.N. Interim Force in Lebanon, said that most of the U.N. force was involved with the search, which included helicopters. "We are getting substantial help from Amal," he said.

All roads in the area had been blocked, Goksell said, and Amal was said to be patrolling a 300-square-mile area in a manhunt for Rich. In Tyre, Daoud Daoud, the Amal military commander for south Lebanon, with whom Rich had met on numerous occasions, said that his militiamen were conducting a door-to-door search for Rich. He said that he was prepared for a military confrontation with the kidnappers, but hoped for "a quick, happy ending."

While boarding Air Force One to return from a vacation in California, President Reagan said, "We're still investigating, trying to learn more about it."

U.N. Secretary General Javier Perez de Cuellar, then traveling in Africa, expressed "profound concern," a U.N. spokesman in New York said. U.N. Undersecretary General Marrack Goulding, then traveling in the Middle East, began diplomatic efforts to gain Rich's release.

As every police officer knows, the first three hours after a crime are the most crucial, and the longer a search is delayed, the lower its chances of success. The search by UNTSO squads went slowly, because in order to cross borders and boundaries they had to request permission from a number of civilian, military, and governmental entities, including U.N. Headquarters in New York, all of which consumed precious time. Amal forces continued to aggressively search southern Lebanon, but few details of their efforts reached us in Washington. UNIFIL helicopters joined the search, but weather problems resulted in their being grounded for two hours in mid-morning. Major Mike Sullivan, on the ground during the search, later said, "You can be sure if they were Marine helicopters, they would've been flying, no matter what!"

Rich's abductors were believed to be the Hezbollah. They claimed that Rich was taken because he was a CIA agent working as a spy for Israel. They had made such threats before. The day Rich was abducted, a Hezbollah note delivered to a news agency in Beirut accused two U.N. Relief and Works Agency members, Jan Stening of Sweden and William Joergensen of Norway, of being "involved in activities of an intelligence service linked to a foreign country." The statement went on to say that the two would be released only "when they are proven innocent."

The effect of the announcement and its timing were chilling for me. Americans were still haunted by the helplessness of their government when in March 1984, William Buckley, the American CIA station chief in Beirut, was captured, interrogated, tortured, and murdered by Shi'ite Muslim extremists. The U.S. government was widely criticized at the time for letting a man who knew such highly classified information be stationed in an area where he was vulnerable to kidnapping.

Sir Brian Urquhart, then the recently retired U.N. Undersecretary General, said the UNTSO officers "serve as the ears and eyes of UNIFIL, and their duties are highly risky." He said Rich was completely aware of the risks that he — or any other commander of the Observation Group Lebanon — would be taking when he accepted the assignment; it was his duty. Could he have been implying it was Rich's duty to be captured?

Karsten Tveit, a Norwegian television correspondent who had traveled with Rich on an assignment, said of Rich, "He felt that he could handle the situation. I was with him without an armed car, and he had no weapons. We were traveling around in the southern part of Lebanon, and he was aware of the risks. He said, 'We can be shot at. We can be robbed, but this is a part of our daily life'." The journalist also stated that as OGL commander, Rich expressed an interest in the pro-Iranian Hezbollah forces and reports that the faction was increasing its activities in southern Lebanon. "He was eager to find out how strong they were," Tveit said. Could he have been implying it was Rich's foolhardiness which brought on this event?

Day 3
February 19, 1988

Two days after Rich's disappearance, an anonymous caller to a news agency in West Beirut claimed that Rich had been abducted by the "Islamic Revolutionary Brigades." Speaking in Arabic, the caller said, "William Higgins has joined the other [foreign] hostages. He will only come out after he is tried on grounds that he is one of the main directors of the CIA in South Lebanon." The man also said that he was

being held neither in Beirut nor in South Lebanon. This claim was not accompanied by any proof, but the caller said that a statement and a photograph of Colonel Higgins would be released soon.

The same day, a Hezbollah faction calling itself "The Organization of the Oppressed of the Earth" delivered a communique typed in Arabic to a Western news agency in Beirut. "We have caught the throat of the American serpent, criminal agent of the satanic CIA and one of the biggest spies, sowing daily terror in our land," the statement read. They claimed responsibility for the kidnapping and included a photocopy of Rich's U.N. identification card. The U.N. verified that the card number matched their records. A cold chill went through my heart. Now I knew beyond any doubt: Rich was a prisoner of war.

"William Higgins, agent of the Central Intelligence Agency, who uses his observer's work as cover for his dangerous espionage role, is in the hands of our heroic warriors," they wrote. The terrorists demanded an end to U.S. intervention in Lebanon, the withdrawal of Israeli troops from southern Lebanon, and the release of 300 to 400 Lebanese and Palestinian prisoners from the Israeli detention camp at Al Khiyam, a village in southern Lebanon within the Israeli "security zone." The enclave, located just north of the border with Israel, is patrolled by about 1,000 Israeli soldiers and Christian Lebanese militiamen of the South Lebanon Army.

The terrorists' demands were remarkably similar to those laid down by the hijackers of a TWA flight in June 1985. During that incident, the passengers were held hostage for nearly three weeks. The same terrorists killed three Lebanese Jews in December 1986. At the time Rich was captured, two of the TWA hijackers were being tried in West Germany, and terrorists captured two Germans as hostages in retaliation. Could it be that Rich's capture was somehow related to that?

More reports came in. In Tyre, Amal militia had supposedly arrested six Hezbollah activists in a raid on a house. The six were accused of having a role in the kidnapping — but nothing else was ever heard about these men.

Many people who heard of Rich's capture were surprised to learn that any Americans were still in southern Lebanon. The widespread assumption was that all official Americans had cleared out of Muslim-controlled areas after the wave of kidnappings which swept Beirut in 1985. Others reflected on the William Buckley fiasco and questioned why Rich, who was coming straight from a Pentagon assignment, would be permitted into a high- danger zone like Lebanon, where he would be an inviting target for terrorists.

Some commentators implied that Rich's presence in Lebanon was somehow an act of negligence on the part of his government — or even his own fault. Others ignored his role as commander of a peacekeeping unit and instead focused solely on his Marine background.

The day after his abduction, the State Department made clear Rich's official status, and distinguished between ordinary Americans told to get out of Lebanon and men like Rich, whose official duties required them to be there. "This U.S. officer was under the responsibility, authority and control of the United Nations in his role as a member of the United Nations Truce Supervisory Organization," State Department spokesman Chuck Redman stated. He stressed that there was no link between the Pentagon and the UNTSO's mission. "These people [the UNTSO] are not under our operational control at all," Redmond said.

Much to my dismay — and later horror — some of the most irresponsible statements came from the last place I'd ever suspect: the U.N.'s own official spokesman in southern Lebanon, Timor Goksell. On the day after Rich's disappearance, Goksell was asked by a newsman how an unarmed American Marine could have ventured into such dangerous territory. "I do share your concern," Goksell replied. "Some of the officers get carried away. They hate to be confined to their bases all the time." Rich had a reputation of being "a bit unusual" because he had moved around the area quite a lot since he was assigned to the region in July, Goksell stated. As if this weren't bad enough, Goksell made another damning statement to the press. "When Colonel Higgins was seized, he was violating U.N. rules for travel by Americans in dangerous areas," Goksell said, but the colonel "felt he couldn't abide by these restrictions... American members of U.N. forces are restricted to the headquarters area and are permitted to travel in Lebanon only with a U.N. military escort."

Goksell clearly didn't know what he was talking about. Rich, a stickler for operational details, had been following out his orders to the letter while commanding UNTSO. When I heard Goksell's outrageous statements, I was stunned — but I held my tongue and said nothing. Rich hadn't gotten "carried away." He was doing exactly the job he was assigned to do, in the way he was expected to do it. It wasn't "unusual" for the commander of the U.N. Truce Supervisory Organization to "move around the area quite a lot." It was his one and only job.

With irresponsible statements flying right and left, damage control became a full-time job for State Department and Pentagon press officers in the days to follow. When a news report erroneously labeled Rich as a "top Pentagon man in Lebanon," a Defense Department official quickly replied, "He's not working for the Pentagon. He's an unarmed U.N. asset whose pedigree just happens to read, 'U.S. Marine Corps.' "

These inaccurate media reports stung me, but nothing that could appear in the press could rouse my emotions like the loss of my husband had. Compared to that loss, and to the overwhelming need to concentrate on bringing him home, the media reports were small concerns to me. I resolved that reacting to them could not get in the way of doing what I needed to do: focus on staying calm, caring for Chrissy, and bringing Rich home.

I learned that my spokesman and now my good friend Commander Bob Prucha had told reporters that Chrissy and I were "hanging in there real well," and that we were "two tough ladies." On that grim day, his characterization of us came as close as possible to making me feel good.

☆☆☆

Day 4
February 20, 1988

On Saturday, Chrissy and I, accompanied by the ever-present and protective Bob Prucha, left our Washington cocoon to attend the funeral of Rich's father in Louisville. Stricken family and friends were grieving as much for Rich as they were for his dad.

**People came to the funeral who had been friends of
Rich and never knew his dad. They came to honor
their friend by paying their respects to his father. The
family, diminished by the past days' events, found
ourselves feeling that maybe Bill Higgins, knowing he
was not strong enough to guide his family through
this, let his life ebb away at this moment in order to
bring us together in this time of need.**

The press was there, but whether because Prucha worked his
magic or they felt otherwise restrained, they left us alone for the most
part. The Commandant of the Marine Corps, General Gray, a good friend
of Rich, sent Brigadier General Edmund Looney as his representative.
Rich's sisters and their preacher felt the warmth as General Looney
quietly and by rote uttered the words to every hymn that was sung and
every Biblical passage that was read. General Looney and I were to
become very good friends starting on that day.

A story in The Boston Globe revealed that Rich had been a high-
level aide to Secretary of Defense Caspar Weinberger. The article
speculated that Rich's access to classified information might have made
his assignment to Lebanon especially risky. My boss, Dan Howard,
replied, "There are no restrictions on where middle-grade officers like
Lieutenant Colonel Higgins can be assigned following Pentagon duty.
His understanding of politico-military affairs and his administrative
abilities made him well-suited for the position in Lebanon."

☆☆☆

Day 5
February 21, 1988

**Since that dreadful moment in the Pentagon briefing
room when I learned that Rich had been kidnapped,
he was never out of my mind for even a moment.
Before I went to bed on Sunday night, I wrote my first
letter to Rich. There was no place to send it, so I wrote**

it on a clean yellow pad, the beginnings of a personal journal:

It's 0343 there. Are you sleeping? I hope you are; you need your sleep, you need your strength. This is what you've been training for all your life; you will get out of it.

Do you know what has been going on here? How can I find the right words to explain it to you? People are mobilizing — powerful people, prayerful people, people who love you, people who don't even know you. The media haven't bothered me. The media are a very superficial media in themselves, and a picture and a story can't come anywhere near capturing the feelings and emotions we are all feeling now.

There is a reason for all of this to be happening. You have said it many times — one man can make a difference. People who haven't spoken for years are speaking; people who haven't aligned themselves are joining the struggle; people who haven't prayed now are praying.

Richard, I feel I am communing with you. Feel my strength as I feel yours. Chrissy and I are doing well; do not use your efforts to worry about us. Use all your efforts to be an American fighting man; use them to overcome this adversity. We have come too far in our love for each other to ever give it up.

I love you. I know you are strong. You have done and are doing the right thing. Come home to me when you can.

  Love, Robin.

Day 6
February 22, 1988

     My heart nearly stopped beating the next time I saw Rich. I had just come into the office on Monday morning, five days after his capture, when Carl Rochelle, CNN's Pentagon reporter, warned me that a videotape

**delivered by the Hezbollah was about to be shown on
television. I stationed myself in Dan Howard's office to
watch it. With Dan, Bill Harlow, and Bob Prucha, I
prepared myself to see my husband. When the videotape
came, I saw my normally happy, animated Marine
sitting in a gray room, clearly under extreme pressure;
his face unshaven, swollen, and emotionless as he read
an obviously prepared text into camera somewhere in
the Mideast. Wearing a gray-green T-shirt, Rich droned
on: "In order to get me released these demands have
to be met." Many of the statements he read were
written in poor English, a certain giveaway that Rich,
a man with two master's degrees, did not write them.**

The statement by the Hezbollah reiterated the demands that the
U.S. cease its diplomatic role in the Middle East, and that Israel release
all Lebanese prisoners and withdraw their forces from southern Lebanon.
After the terrorists' 70-second video was played, both White House and
State Department spokesmen immediately pointed out to viewers that all
statements made by hostages are made under duress.

At the same moment, Amal was stepping up their dragnet search
of Lebanon — a move which was violently denounced by pro-Iranian
Muslim religious leaders. The mullahs condemned Amal's search for
Rich, backed the Hezbollah demands for release of Lebanese and
Palestinian prisoners, and reaffirmed their allegiance to the tyrannical
Iranian leader, Ayatollah Ruhollah Khomeini. An Amal representative
accused the Hezbollah kidnappers of being motivated not by fears of
spies but for the money. "Kidnapping operations which have targeted
foreigners in Beirut under the slogan of combating espionage soon wind
down to money deals," an Amal spokesman said. "Vast amounts of cash
are distributed among various factions."

A major break in the case — or so it appeared to us — came on
February 24th. Daoud Daoud, commander of the Amal militia in the Tyre
area, confirmed that two of Rich's abductors, as well as a third man who
was carrying a letter from Beirut to the kidnappers with orders to bring
Rich to the Lebanese capital, had been arrested. The three denied knowing
the whereabouts of their leader or where Rich was being held prisoner.

According to Amal sources, the kidnapping was a "masterpiece from a professional standpoint." A security source who spoke to an Associated Press reporter said that "the mastermind used five identical brown Volvo cars plus two additional getaway cars, a white Peugeot and a red Mercedes, in the abduction. The squads in each car did not know who was in the other cars."[3]

Daoud stated that "the kidnappers switched their hostage from a Volvo to a pickup truck, then to a Mercedes 280, and then the trail was lost."[4]

Daoud also stated that Amal knew the name of the mastermind of the plot, but neither his name nor those of the other three were released at that time.

By the time ten days had passed with no progress toward Rich's release, my body was thoroughly exhausted and my mind deeply distressed. The strain of keeping a stiff upper lip was rapidly wearing me out. In Jerusalem, Secretary of State George Schultz began a round of diplomacy on February 26, shuttling between the offices of Israeli Prime Minister Yitzhak Shamir and his political opponent, Foreign Minister Shimon Peres. At the same time in Muslim West Beirut, 10,000 pro-Iranian Lebanese Shi'ite militants protested Schultz's Middle Eastern tour by marching through the streets and calling for Rich's execution.

A Muslim protester set fire to a gasoline-soaked American flag, which he waved through the air on the end of a stick. Behind him, a turbaned protester screamed through a bullhorn, "The masses of our nation have spoken today. Let this spy Higgins be executed. Death to Higgins!"

The crowd roared its approval. "Death to Higgins! Death to the filthy spy! Death to America, the Great Satan." That night I went to bed with the sound of the enraged mob ringing in my ears. I prayed to God for the strength I'd need to get through the next day. The miracle I received was the last one I expected that night: sleep.

---

[3] Hasan Mroue, Associated Press, "Amal's Higgins Search Nets 3 Abductors, Who Play Dumb," *Washington Times*, February 24, 1988.
[4] Nora Boustany, "3 Kidnappers of Marine Arrested," *The Washington Post*, February 24, 1988.

Last known photo of Rich taken before he was captured, on observation post, South Lebanon, early 1988

Chapter 7

I Never Married a Cowboy

Day 12
February 29, 1988

Two weeks after his abduction, I had no idea whether my husband was dead or alive. Rumors and speculation abounded, but hard evidence was nowhere to be found. The United Nations had done nothing to start an official investigation, so I was completely in the dark. I had no idea how long I would have to wait to hear anything reliable. Looking back, I know it's best that I didn't know.

By early 1988, a couple dozen Westerners had been kidnapped in Lebanon. At the time that Rich was kidnapped, eight other Americans were being held hostage. As the occasional hostage was released or escaped, the details of his treatment by this radical group slowly became known.

Jeremy Levin, a journalist, was held in solitary confinement for months. He told of being bound with a short chain to a wall so he could only lie down or sit up. He was blindfolded, physically abused, and given little to eat.

Father Lawrence Martin Jenco, a Roman Catholic priest, was kidnapped January 8, 1985, and released July 26, 1986. He wrote of his six months in solitary confinement: "The first thing you do upon being captured is sing. Then you cry. And, finally, you remain silent." The priest kept track of time by marking days with saliva in the dust on his prison walls. He marked the months by tying knots in the fringe of a potato sack. One day, his captors tied explosives to his body. Another time, he saw a chain suspended from a ceiling and thought he was about to be executed. Although his faith never wavered, he admitted that he told God, "I'm not Job. I want to go home now."

Charles Glass, an ABC journalist, was blindfolded, his hands and feet shackled to a wall. As I read and listened to the former hostages' accounts, I became progressively more concerned about Rich's welfare.

However, I now had to worry myself with more insidious phenomena. There was so much bickering and armchair debating and finger-pointing going on in the press, that I wondered whether or not anyone cared that an American patriot could at this very moment be dying for his country.

Over the years a general perception grew among the American public that the U.S. government must have a plan for informing and counseling the families of prisoners of war (POWs) or civilian hostages taken overseas. One by one, the POW and hostage families of the Korean War, Vietnam War, and the Middle Eastern crisis learned the truth. The U.S. government has no plan. Every hostage family has to fight for information, plead for or demand action, and fend for itself. For certain, there are friends, family and fellow sufferers who may lend a sympathetic ear or helping hand, but it is rarely the government who is there to help or inform. POW and hostage families each have to find their own ways to cope.

One of the most difficult issues that a POW's or hostage's family must deal with is the heinous tendency of those who should know better — or those engaged in idle speculation — to blame the victim, rather than his captors, for the victim's plight.

Within hours of his kidnapping, accusations started circulating that Rich or his government — rather than the terrorists — might somehow be responsible for creating the problem. Loose-lipped U.N.

officials and shoot-from-the-hip journalists portrayed Rich as a foolhardy, boastful, reckless man — and maybe even a CIA spy — who might have put himself at needless risk. Worse, none of them seemed to learn from their mistakes. The news media, in particular, kept dredging up and repeating old, baseless rumors and discredited statements. Perhaps they believed it made better press and sold more papers.

I soon found out that, like other POW and hostage families, I had to deal not only with the kidnapping and imprisonment of my husband, but with the gnawing fear that people might come to think that Rich's capture was somehow his own fault, thereby lessening their resolve to get him home.

In January 1987, because of the growing violence there, Secretary of State George Schultz restricted the use of U.S. passports for travel to, through, or in Lebanon. This is the closest thing he could do to ordering Americans out of the country. At the time of Rich's kidnapping, eight American civilians, three British, four French, and ten other foreign nationals were being held hostage in Lebanon. The American Embassy made it clear that Lebanon was no longer a safe place for American civilians.

In the United States, most Americans probably thought that all U.S. citizens left Lebanon after the travel ban, but this was not the case. Even after the ban went into effect, some American civilians remained for personal reasons, despite the repeated urgings of U.S. officials to leave. They knew the danger of kidnapping — and chose to stay nonetheless.

In compliance with long-standing agreements, U.S. troops had continued to work with the U.N. peacekeeping forces. Men like Rich and other American military members continued to be assigned to UNTSO. It was their official duty to be in Lebanon, and they were there under government orders.

In Tyre, Lebanon, two days after Rich's capture, Aly Yassin, a fundamentalist Shi'ite religious leader, speculated that Rich had been targeted for abduction "primarily because he was an American, not because he was a member of a U.N.-affiliated organization."[5]

---

[5] Nora Boustany, "U.N., Amal Forces Fail To Find Kidnapped U.S. Marine Officer," *The Washington Post*, February 19, 1988.

Shortly after his capture, a Hezbollah weekly newspaper, Al Aahd, all but justified Higgins' kidnapping by suggesting that he was as important as another Marine lieutenant colonel who worked for the National Security Council, Oliver L. North.[6]

Here in the United States, the allegation soon arose that, knowing the unique dangers of Lebanon to Americans, the U.S. government was negligent for having put yet another of its citizens in harm's way.

U.S. Senator Malcolm Wallop (R-Wyoming) stated, "I'm exasperated by the idea that we would have an official American presence that was so vulnerable that a hostage could be taken. My point is: If we're going to have high-ranking presence over there that's on official American business, it ought to be protected, and these kinds of things ought not to be possible."

This position ignored the fact that the United States had made a long-term commitment to peace in the region, starting in 1948. From that point forward, U.S. peacekeeping troops had always been a part of the U.N. presence in the region.

The U.N. presence became crucial when the Lebanese civil war broke out in the mid 1970s. At that point, noted Gary Anderson in a column in *The Washington Times*, "the U.N. observers became a symbol of stability in a nation fast descending into chaos."

When the violence in Lebanon escalated in the mid-1980s, the U.S. government expressed its resolve not to throw in the towel and let the terrorists take control and force the United States and the U.N. out. To do so would have been a sign of weakness and a default on our nation's commitment to peacekeeping in the area. Further, it would have subjected the remaining U.N. peacekeepers to higher risk.

"If the U.N. blue beret is no longer a guarantee of freedom of action in a war zone," Anderson wrote, "we have taken a giant step down the dark road toward barbarism in international relations."

In early 1988, of course, I understood little of this. In time I was to become quite a student of the situation and would come to believe that

---

[6] *The Washington Post*, April 14, 1988.

our government's fault was not in being there, but in defaulting authority and command to the U.N. during its stay.

The next statement to raise the public's suspicions and my hackles came from news correspondent Daniel Schorr. He alleged that Rich was assigned to Lebanon "in the face of standing rules against sending officers with recent access to sensitive information into communist or other hazardous areas." Schorr went on to state that "Defense Department regulations were waived which barred officers with current knowledge of top-level security information from travel to any area where he might be at risk."

In fact, neither Secretary Weinberger nor General Colin Powell knew that Rich was applying for the UNTSO job. When they learned that he had been accepted for the assignment, both expressed personal concern about the potential danger. The Army, Marine Corps, Department of Defense, Joint Chiefs of Staff, State Department, and CIA all knew he had been selected, and no one objected. Schorr's statement that rules had been bent in order for a man with recent, highly classified knowledge to be posted to Lebanon was perhaps based on logic, but was not accurate. For months, Rich himself wondered if his high-level Pentagon background would disqualify him for the UNTSO post. No one ever questioned, ever stopped him.

As it turned out, Lebanon was not on the list of dangerous posts for which a man with his knowledge would have been barred. No waiver of the rules was necessary for the assignment. The Lebanon post was classified as "unrestricted," even though its being omitted from the list of dangerous spots may well have been an oversight by someone in the government.

However, what galled me even more than Schorr's academic, albeit inaccurate, public dissertation was that he himself was highlighting Rich's importance to the very people who were just waiting to learn what kind of a catch they had. While Daniel Schorr, and then other reporters, like *The Washington Post's* Molly Moore and ABC's Bob Zellnick, found this line of argument tantalizing, Rich Higgins' captors were learning from Rich's own countrymen that they had really struck gold. Years later I had the opportunity to share my distress over this reporting with Mr. Schorr who, ironically, often speaks about responsibility and ethics in journalism. He apologized and confided in me that he should have been more circumspect.

Rich was a self-motivated high-achiever. Like any mid-level officer — or corporate manager, for that matter — Rich wanted to proceed up the career ladder. As a Marine Corps infantry officer, that meant earning the right to command a combat battalion. There is no doubt about it: The UNTSO position was the right assignment at the right time in his career — as it would have been for any other Marine officer in his position. Pentagon officials noted that all thirty-six UNTSO positions allotted to Americans are highly coveted, and that the officers who serve in those posts "have all served in potentially sensitive or high-level jobs prior to winning one."[7]

However, Rich's motives for taking the U.N. position went far beyond simple career aspirations. The post would provide him with the opportunity to get back into the field with a chance to work with soldiers from other nations. In a world of global economies and multinational forces, such experience is vital. Even beyond that, Rich truly believed that one man could make a positive difference in the world. Having personally interviewed Rich earlier in Lebanon, author Rona M. Fields wrote that Rich believed that "the future of the military is peacekeeping." He wanted to be that future.

The attacks on Rich's character started the day after his kidnapping. It horrified me that one of the first came from Timor Goksell, the U.N.'s own spokesman, who described him as a "bit of a cowboy" who "might have gotten carried away." In a story entitled, "The Quagmire Claims a Gung-ho Hostage," *U.S. News and World Report* expanded Goksell's statement, attributing his single remark to "Beirut diplomats."[8] This piece of sloppy writing made it appear that the entire diplomatic corps — and not just Timor Goksell — thought that Rich sought adventure and took unnecessary risks in order to achieve a "tough guy" reputation.

The man who could and should have been Rich's staunchest ally was, in fact, one of his greatest problems. Timor Goksell was the first to blurt out damaging and unfounded statements around which the "cowboy" image coalesced. As the man charged with stating the official position of

---

[7] "Marine Spoke of Past Post, Sources Say," in *The Washington Post*, February 22, 1988.
[8] "The Quagmire Claims a Gung-ho Hostage," *U.S. News & World Report*, February 29, 1988.

the United Nations, Goksell should have talked of the U.N.'s outrage and commitment to get Rich — one of their senior officers on the scene — repatriated at all costs. Instead, Goksell's conduct strengthened the hand of Rich's captors by deflecting blame from the hostage-takers to the hostage.

Why would the U.N. spokesman say such things about a man whose life was at stake? I was told that Rich's aggressive management of OGL had angered some of the U.N.'s "old hands," Goksell among them. Many UNIFIL and UNTSO officials had carved out comfortable lives in Israel, where they and their families spent their time shopping in the Arab souks, or markets, relatively untouched by the chaos swirling around them. They stayed in safe areas, took no risks, and rocked no boats.

When, the day after the kidnapping, Goksell pronounced from his office in Jerusalem that Rich had a reputation for being "a bit unusual" because he had moved around the area quite a lot, I was shocked and incensed. Rich knew that he had an important job to do and went out into the middle of the fray and observed. It's what real observers do. It also made the U.N. do-nothing, headquarters bureaucrats look bad by comparison. Some of them took their revenge through rumormongering. Under other circumstances, Goksell's irresponsible, off-the-cuff statements might simply have been dismissed as unprofessional, but with a U.N. officer's life at stake, Goksell's statements were unconscionable.

Back at home, Daniel Schorr continued to add to the problem. Without offering any proof or naming any source of the statement, Schorr claimed that Rich "boasted of his Weinberger connection to his 75-man multinational detachment."[9]

First-hand observers and those who served with Rich painted quite a different picture. They saw him as an energetic, professional officer who built trust and inspired confidence. There was no doubt he was strongly pro-active in his role of head U.N. peacekeeper in Lebanon, but those who actually saw him in action had nothing but praise for his attitude and conduct.

David Evans, a Marine lieutenant colonel who had served with Rich in the Pentagon, later a columnist for the *Chicago Tribune*, stated unequivocally that Rich's image was "hardly the Flashman of Marine

---

[9] Daniel Schorr, "Another Target Sent to Lebanon," *Cleveland Plain Dealer*, February 29, 1988.

Corps; he's the very opposite... The Marine Corps preaches an activist philosophy of leadership," Evans said. "By training and indoctrination, Higgins was predisposed to assume a vigorous and visible role in his U.N. assignment, traveling throughout the region to maintain a close watch over his troops... Despite the danger of traveling unarmed as a U.N. observer, it was inconceivable for Higgins to remain huddled inside the relative sanctuary of the U.N. compound."[10]

Why was I so positive that Rich wasn't the hot-blooded "cowboy" he was accused of being? Even if I hadn't been his wife, best friend and comrade-in-arms for over ten years, I was still his penpal. Like many Marine officers, Rich wasn't overly demonstrative in public, yet he was very communicative and introspective when he put pen to paper. A letter he wrote to me three months before painted a very clear picture of the commander of the Observer Group Lebanon. The picture was of a disciplined, self-assured man who felt he had the confidence of his U.N. superiors and a mandate to carry out his responsibilities. On October 10, 1987, Rich had written to me:

> *Because of the action in the Gulf, there have been new threats from Iran and the Hezbollah. I think they are shallow or will not include U.N. people. The Americans are restricted, as they should be, so I am sure they will not be returned to full duty — and I believe that is correct. However, a decision has been made that the "Chief is the Chief" and will have full access and support of the U.N.*
>
> *I spent the last two days patrolling in Shi'ite villages that are mostly Hezbollah. Strangely enough, I received no great hostility and they seemed to be accepting of the fact that we would be meeting together. I feel the danger of the environment — but I am strangely confident and comfortable. I shall be careful but I shall be firm in pursuing my obligations as the Chief...*
>
> *We finished the day yesterday with a small firefight along the AOL and began today with an Israeli assault about 400 meters from the U.N. position. I still am not*

---

[10] David Evans, "Higgins' Critics Are Unfair To This Energetic Marine," *Chicago Tribune*, February 26, 1988.

sure what they were doing. But the day is beautiful. The
countryside is beautiful. The Galilee is as wonderful as I
have always read. And I miss you. Thanks for letting me
be a soldier one more time. I love you for it.

Rich

Perhaps President Ronald Reagan summed it up best: "It's a dangerous business to begin with," he observed at a news conference, "and this particular officer happened to volunteer when there was a vacancy."

The next allegation to come down was that Rich had violated U.N. security procedures by riding alone in the car. This would have been true — if he had not been in a convoy with another vehicle. U.N. security regulations did not require that Rich have an extra person with him in his car, as long as he was traveling in a convoy, which he was. The two men in the lead Jeep were there because Rich was precisely following the U.N.'s Standard Operating Procedures. Having a passenger in his own Jeep would have accomplished little of value, since an attack upon the car would likely have been to get Rich because he was the Chief of OGL. Having another unarmed officer as a passenger would only have endangered the passenger, while not making the Chief any more secure. Rich would not have needlessly used and endangered one of his men that way.

Major Mike Sullivan, who served with him in Lebanon, knew Rich well. "From the day he took over, he developed a training program centered around security awareness," Sullivan said in an interview with the Navy Times. "He worried most that a U.N. observer would be kidnapped and he insisted that everyone know emergency procedures... He won the hearts and minds of the OGL families. Their welfare was on top of his list, with training a close second. He set a pace a lot of observers hadn't experienced before... Higgins believed everybody was at risk as soon as they crossed the border into Lebanon, "so he pounded on precautionary steps," Sullivan said. "This may sound trite, but I admire everything about the man, not only as an officer and leader, but as a human. He made a positive impact over there."[11]

---

[11] Mel Jones, "Peacekeeper Won The Hearts and Minds of His Charges," *Navy Times*, November 7, 1988.

It was said that U.N. regulations barred American OGL officers from traveling in dangerous areas within Lebanon, but this was also a half-truth. The American contingent of OGL was largely confined to duties within their headquarters compound, but it was the responsibility of the Chief to personally instruct and inspect the work of all his observers throughout his command area. In visiting them, Rich wasn't being reckless, just doing his job and taking the same risks as his men.

The claim by the Hezbollah that Rich was a spy for the CIA was simply their justification for having kidnapped him in the first place. The Lebanese with whom Rich had come into contact viewed him with a mixture of admiration and suspicion. An American in Lebanon is always an object of curiosity, all the more so an American commanding a multinational military force. Lebanese who met Higgins on one of his frequent tours of outposts say they assumed he was important to the American government or he would never have been sent to Lebanon. Since they knew that Americans were ordinarily forbidden to enter their country, they assumed that anyone who did so, and with the support of the American government at that, must be a spy.

Was Rich a spy? No. He was a lieutenant colonel in the Marine Corps on an assignment with the United Nations. He had no CIA ties or training. But radical factions like the Hezbollah consider any American who crosses borders into Lebanon, from Israel, who lives in Israel, consorts with Israelis, to be a spy for Israel. There is no way to convince them otherwise.

It didn't help at all when in April 1988, the Washington journal, *American Politics*, published an unsubstantiated, unsourced report which gave credence to the captors' justification. The article (which, had it been published in wartime, might have subjected the author to arrest for treason), stated, "The word going around spook circles in Washington is that Marine Lieutenant Colonel William Higgins was doing a little more than just putting in time with the U.N. Truce Supervision Organization in southern Lebanon when he was snatched by Shi'ite crazies. Let's put it this way: During the height of the Cold War in the '50s, reliable sources have estimated that more than half of the CIA's field agents were active-duty military personnel. And some people say that since that '50s kind of guy, Ronald Reagan, came to town, the '80s started to look more and more like those good old days of three decades ago."[12] All I could think when I read this piece of inflammatory gossip was: Don't these writers know that what they are saying here in this flippant manner could result in the death of my husband?

But perhaps one of the most hurtful attacks on Rich was from a fellow Marine officer. An unnamed-by-the-media personnel officer — whom I knew to be a lieutenant colonel jealous at the attention Rich had gotten in previous assignments and that Rich had been cleared to go to Lebanon over his objections because he wanted him to go to a more menial assignment — spoke with the press and added unfounded attacks on Rich's character. "Good for him" he snapped in a *Washington Post* article. That totally deflated me; all my career Rich and others told me Marines stick together.

What could I say to those who were critical of him and his role, and to Rich's captors? I wanted to defend Rich. But he was the officer I admired most, and he would have known what I should say or not say had he been here. But I could say what I felt and that is that he was there doing a job, doing it the best he knew how as a Marine Corps officer. Regardless of what the news was saying — he was not a "cowboy." That hurt me and made me angry. Anyone who knew him knew that was not true. It hurt because he was not there to defend himself; though, in fact, if he had been, he would not have defended himself. He did not do that. He was the most gentle, the most kind, the most unselfish man I knew. He believed in peace. Yes, he volunteered — I venture to say if any Marine had been given the opportunity to have a job like that he would have volunteered. Peacekeeping is hard, as Marines know so well, but leadership and command in a combat environment is a Siren's call to any Marine who believes one man can make a difference.

The incessant flow of stories and rumors which nipped at the heels of Rich's professional reputation and suggested that somehow he had brought his kidnapping on himself continued to hurt and anger me. I desperately wanted to respond to the media in defense of Rich, but I decided that his image would be better defended by those who knew him well — and could not be accused of simply defending our family name. Instead of mounting a high-profile personal media barrage — a step for

---

[12] *American Politics*, April 1988.

which I was professionally trained and capable — I preferred instead to urge Rich's many colleagues and superiors to set the record straight through their own statements. Over the succeeding months, they did just that. I saved my energy for staying in close touch with my official and unofficial contacts in the State Department, Department of Defense, and the United Nations, urging them to put pressure on those who were perpetuating unfounded rumors.

I went to my job at the Pentagon each day, and for eight hours tried to maintain some semblance of being a professional information officer. During the day, I threw myself into my work. This helped me keep my mind off the inescapable reality which pervaded my consciousness: Rich was a hostage, and there was little I could do about it.

Evenings were much harder. I spent them writing letters to Rich that I recorded in my personal journal, for there was no address to send them to. I also made many phone calls to family, all designed to give me the simple comforts of personal contact that Rich's capture had now denied me. Most of all, I felt that the more comfortable they were with the information I was providing them, the less likely they'd be to speak with the press and to speculate. There was enough damage being done in Washington. It seemed to work, and my efforts with the family kept the official Higgins' response with me and me alone.

Meanwhile, except for the continuing family contacts, I found I became less interested in returning calls to the hundreds of friends and long-lost relatives who all wanted to get close to me and to be my best friends. I had enough of talking to people. I became a bit of a hermit.

Talking became an exhausting chore, so I began to surround myself with only a small, close circle of friends. I came to call them "my bubba group."

The nights were long; I slept little, and then only fitfully. Every time that I started to drift into despair over the next rumor or unfounded statement, Rich would come to me and say: Remember, a true leader leads from the front. And when you're out front, people will shoot at you. Those little phrases which I had always thought made Rich sound a bit quixotic now became the mantras of my sanity.

Chapter 8

The High Price of Heritage

Day 14
March 1, 1988

**With my husband in the hands of Islamic fundamentalist
fanatics, one of the most harrowing aspects of my life
was my fear that the Hezbollah would somehow discover
that the wife of their newest hostage was a Jew. The
Hezbollah were fanatically committed to the destruction
of the Jewish state, its supporters (especially the United
States), and to the extermination of Jews. I didn't want
Rich to be seen as an Israeli sympathizer, because they
treat Israeli prisoners very harshly.**

I also knew that if the U.S. State Department or anyone else —
and, God forbid, the United Nations — knew I was Jewish, it could be
yet another excuse to say the matter was too difficult and out of their
hands. I wanted to ensure that Rich was seen solely as an American
officer in the active service of the United Nations and nothing else.

I decided that the best thing, indeed, the only thing for me to do was to suppress all evidence that I was Jewish. I believed the tragic irony was that the one thing besides my husband that meant the most to me, that made me who I am — my faith — could in fact be the single most damaging piece of information which could fall into the enemy's hands.

The need to repress all information about my heritage pained me deeply, for I had started to cherish my Jewishness since my first trip to Israel as a college student. Since that time, my bonding with my faith had continued to grow. But I immediately focused on the reality of the situation. The Hezbollah were the sworn enemies of Jews everywhere, and were committed to the destruction of the Jewish state. I remembered the old security slogan which was immortalized by the government during World War II: "Loose Lips Sink Ships." I knew that the threats to Rich's life would increase dramatically if it became known that he was married to a Jew.

Rich should never have married me! Being married to me could hurt him more than any other single thing! It's my fault he's in the predicament he is! It was up to me to prevent that piece of information from getting out; I had to prevent that at any cost. I had to become not a Jew.

My immediate concern was that, thinking they were doing something helpful, a friend or family member would inadvertently let that crucial piece of information slip. I began to develop my own media plan based upon my experiences and now-extensive reading on pertinent issues. I continued to distance myself from friends — if they didn't know what I was going through, they wouldn't have enough information to speak with the press and they wouldn't let the information slip.

I was most concerned about my father. He and my mother had divorced years ago, and the press hadn't yet found my mother in San Francisco. Anyway, although she desperately wanted to reach out to me, she was a private person, unaccustomed to and uninterested in speaking publicly. In south Florida, my father also wanted so badly to help, to be there for me, and the press was all around him once they found him. He was eager to speak with the press, and he was certainly capable of putting into words our distress.

But he was Jewish – he and his wife had New York accents like all the other Jewish retirees from New York; they sprinkled Yiddish words and phrases in their conversation; they lived in a predominantly Jewish retirement community; they had a mezuzah on their doorpost and Jewish symbols around the house. I had several heated conversations with my father about the need to either stop talking publicly or to remove Jewish symbols from his house. Our passions began to get the best of us for a while until we realized how much we needed each other at this time. He also, I later understood, had a conversation with his rabbi, who explained to him about *pikuah nefesh*, that is, the understanding of the breaking of certain religious dictum in order to preserve life. This was a matter of life or death.

My extensive readings on the topic of prisoners of war taught me that friends or family might see no harm in sharing intimate details with the press; she or he may think their friend, neighbor or loved one will come home faster if they go on television and appeal to those who hold a hostage by saying Aunt So-And-So is dying or little brother Such-And-Such misses him. I was intrigued and took to heart an article written by L. Paul Bremer, III, then Ambassador-at-Large for Counter-Terrorism at the State Department. I was later to meet him and get a more personal and less inspirational outlook, but his article was apt. It pointed out that prisoners often misrepresent their marital status, professional responsibilities, career histories, and other personal facts in their efforts to secure better treatment or bring about their release. "One former hostage," he said in the article, "is certain that the lies the prisoner told his captors saved his life."[13]

Facts about prisoners and others missing in action revealed or verified by family members could have deadly consequences. As a Pentagon press officer, I knew this was true. For that reason, the possibility of an inadvertent news leak haunted me. Everything became private. I became reclusive. I was afraid of anything that the press might pick up.

Family and friends aside, my greatest concern was that the press would find out and, as they had so many other times in Rich's case, release news of my religion — a seemingly small piece of potentially

---

[13] L. Paul Bremer, III, "Terrorism, The Media, And The Government," *Parameters: Journal of the U.S. Army War College*, March 1988.

lethal information — without thinking of its implications to Rich's safety. It just plain would make great news – it would thicken the plot.

I also knew that reporters are normal human beings, with their own sensitivities and feelings, but they are a very persistent group. When it comes to reporting a breaking story or scooping other networks or papers, they can become ruthless. If you are the "story de jour," they will check in phone books and call your family and your neighbors and your co-workers. They will visit your children at school, and they will talk with your children's friends. They will call any time of the day or night, and they will insist that the American people have a right to know your deepest feelings. I knew that before and came to live it. One morning, for example, 17-year-old Chrissy was awakened at 6:00 A.M. by a stranger on the phone wanting to know what her response was to a news report just received that her father would be executed. After that, I had our phone number changed and unlisted.

The media thrive on controversy, and they will insist your family owes it to the American public to speak out. They are interested in anything and are especially interested in sensational details — such as criticism of the military or the government. All this comes at the worst possible time for a family in crisis, who are under intense stress and may not be thinking clearly. I refused to let this happen to me. I was thinking very clearly — and I stopped talking to friends, to family, and, most of all, to press.

Of course, there were others — family members like Peggy Say, Terry Anderson's sister, for example — who were extremely outspoken. Evidently, her experience told her the exact opposite — the more she spoke out about her brother, the better she felt about her ability to effect his release.

When a natural but not uncommon disaster such as a hurricane or tornado strikes, the community knows how to respond. The Red Cross trucks roll out to the disaster area. The community implements its disaster plan. Government-run shelters are opened and staffed. The Federal Emergency Management Agency sends generators and mobile homes. Banks start accepting and channeling funds for relief efforts. In 1988, when a family member was kidnapped by terrorists in the Middle East, there was no equivalent community response. People express shock and concern, but don't know how to act or what to say. Should they attempt to console the family — thereby implying that the hostage may not come home? Or try to raise their spirits, imparting what may be unfounded hope and optimism that the hostage will soon be freed? It's no wonder that some hostage families soon felt abandoned, for nothing in the world prepares one — or one's friends — for facing the crushing ambiguities of life as a hostage's family member and loved one.

Luckily, Marines and their families over the years understood that loved ones might disappear and never come home. Those men and women who lived through the uncertainties of Vietnam tried to recall how they bonded together. The Marine family tried to rally around me. But this was not war, Rich was the only one, and "hostage" was an unclear word to those of us in the military community.

As the days and weeks dragged on, I saw less and less of my casual friends and more of a few close ones. In the first few days of the crisis I realized that if I were going to be effective in influencing Rich's release, I'd need the active help and support of the best minds I could possibly bring to bear on the situation. With this in mind, I organized my "bubba group": an inner circle of trusted and endeared advisors whose contacts spread into all the branches of the military and the government. I learned that term from Rich, my very own "good-ole-boy" from the South.

The group's makeup changed over time, but the core group of "my bubbas" included Colonel Tom Harkins, a Marine colonel and a Middle East expert who had served in Beirut during the early 80s; Harry Klein, a former Army officer who was widely respected as one of the foremost experts in counter-terrorism and Middle East intelligence analysts; Colonel Fred Hof, a brilliant Army officer and assistant to Rich Armitage, Assistant Secretary of Defense for International Security Affairs; Major Kathy Wood, an Army public affairs officer whom I nicknamed "coach," my media spokesman and advisor; and later Greg Craig, a young, enthusiastic, and innovative lawyer with the noted Washington law firm of Williams and Connelly.

My bubbas were among the very few people who understood me and my mission. For this reason, they were also the only people from whom I was able to feel real support. They listened and commented on my ideas, shared ideas and information, spoke with their respective bosses, and helped me strategize my positions. They were as convinced of the value of my mission and as focused on its success as I was. In those months of constant horror and chaos, they were my lifeline to sanity.

On April 5, Kuwaiti Flight 422 was hijacked by Arab terrorists, and the affair took on a special relevance for me. The jet was commandeered in Larnaca, Cyprus, by Islamic fundamentalists. In Lebanon, the Organization of the Oppressed on Earth threatened to hang Rich if local authorities tried to storm the plane. I avoided the press, who all wanted a comment. Two weeks later, after killing two hostages and holding the rest of the crew and passengers captive, the Iranian-backed hijackers abandoned the airplane in Algeria. I didn't hear another word about Rich.

April 19 brought even worse news. The Voice of Lebanon, a Christian-controlled radio station in Beirut, reported that Rich had been "killed and buried by his captors" in the village of Siddiquine, 47 miles south of Beirut, during fighting by rival Moslem militias earlier in the month.[14]

Was it over? Was my Rich dead and cold and buried halfway around the world from me? My heart immediately sank into the pit of my stomach. I broke out in a dry sweat, but tried to retain my composure. After all, I told myself, this is just another unsubstantiated rumor. U.S. and U.N. officials said they had no information on the report. But having given myself the pep talk, I still felt cold and empty inside. Again I avoided the press, who again wanted a comment.

Three days after the "dead-and-buried" report, the Hezbollah released a statement saying that Rich would be tried for spying. "This criminal will be turned over today to the Tribunal of the Oppressed to judge him for the crimes he has committed," said the statement.[15]

My heart leapt. I was elated! Rich was alive! He did not die during the Kuwaiti plane hijacking, and he was not buried in Siddiquine! Then the emotional absurdity of it all dawned on me: In effect, I was celebrating the news that Rich would be tried by religious lunatics in a terrorist kangaroo court for a crime of which he had already been convicted. At times like that, it was extremely difficult for me to hold

---

[14] "Lebanese Radio Reported Death of Higgins," *Chicago Tribune*, April 19, 1988.
[15] "Pro-Iran Faction Says It Will Try U.S. Captive," *The New York Times*, April 22, 1988.

onto my sanity. So I did what I found myself doing more and more often. I wrote to Rich in the journal I never mailed:

April 11, 1988

I know you are alive — I also feel things might be getting tough for you. Hold on, they are for me too, but we must be strong together.

Just as I get good feelings and good reports, so today I got the worst one since they called you a CIA spy. Today they said they killed you and buried you at Siddiquine. I must admit that threw me for a loop; but Rich, it's not true, it's disinformation and they're putting it out to confuse us. But I won't let it happen. Just after that one was laid to rest — I talked to Dave Vetter[16] about it, then went down to the DIA [Defense Intelligence Agency] — I got a Reuter's story that said they'd hang you if the Kuwaiti airliner is stormed. Oh, Richard, I love you so, I don't want them to be playing with you like this.

Then DIA threatened to cut me off — I don't know at what level it's coming from, but they can't do this. I have been surprised that so many people have been sharing so much with me, but it's been good and helpful. And they can't cut me off. Tomorrow I'll go see General Perroots[17] if I have to...

God, I want you back so bad. Today a lot happened. Pluses and minuses. But on the whole it's been a negative day. Maybe tomorrow will be positive.

Richard, think of escape. I want you back. Come home to me. I just can't wait. I will always of course, but I sure don't want to!

---

[16] Colonel Dave Vetter, Rich's replacement as military assistant to the Secretary of Defense, a Marine, a friend, and gentle and sweet man.

[17] Lieutenant General Leonard H. Perroots, then the Director of the Defense Intelligence Agency.

I'll love you always.

Two months had passed since Rich had become a prisoner of war. Waves of feelings washed over me as constantly as the waves in the ocean roar to the shore. I wanted Rich to be freed... and more. In one of my hundreds of unsent letters, I wrote to Rich:

> *I want revenge. I want the coordinates of these beasts' houses. I will get them. If they harm you, I will go after them with a vengeance as you would. But no, you will be back. I still believe that, but my world is falling apart fast without you. I built my world around you and rightly so. You are worth it.*

I spent most of my time with the friends and family I still spoke with defusing erroneous rumors and undoing the effects of deliberate disinformation. There was no time for intimacies and other emotions. By the time I got through with what I had to do, I was exhausted.

I soon learned how those clichés we hear so often get started and what they mean:

"I am numb." I found myself holding the trauma all out away from me like a hand mirror. Then it wouldn't really touch me. But it left me out there, and what was left of me was a shell, going through the motions of work and play and not really feeling any of it.

"I live from day to day." I didn't plan for any tomorrows. I resented anyone who asked me to. The reason for that was that I believed it could be tomorrow that he'd be home and my life would change — again — dramatically. I lived one day at a time. I sighed as I woke up and sighed again as I made it to the end of the day. I didn't know what tomorrow would bring — and couldn't control it, anyway. It was not in my hands. I was not used to being so out of control. So I didn't think about tomorrow.

"I'm on an emotional roller-coaster." I started each day at 5:00 A.M. on the highway to Washington. In my solitary hour-long drive, I thought through the day. I gave myself a pep talk, not knowing what would happen. Upon arriving at the Pentagon, I carefully scrutinized the overnight messages, then the morning news clips. That set the tone for the morning, until I got some other stimulus, which I almost always did. My feelings and moods didn't run day by day. They changed constantly. Every moment was different.

What gave me strength? In those early days, Chrissy, Rich's daughter, always daddy's girl, gave me strength. I don't know how she managed it, but she was optimistic and cheerful.

My family and friends gave me strength. They made me proud, they prayed, and they believed in Richard.

The Marine Corps gave me strength. Marines and their families have borne this kind of agony for over two hundred years. I knew that I was not the first. I knew that I was not alone.

Rich gave me strength — his inner strength. I knew that he was morally, physically, and mentally tough. I wanted him to know that I was, too. And that is what I told him every day, all day, and every night, when I wrote him all those letters that could never be mailed.

On April 28, 1988, seventy days after the kidnapping, I met with former Secretary of Defense and Rich's former boss, Caspar Weinberger. He was wonderful. We were quite frank with each other. I told him some of my ideas. He took notes, and said that he would call General Colin Powell, who was then National Security Advisor. I believe he also called Rich Armitage, former Assistant Secretary for International Security Affairs, because I later talked to Mr. Armitage, who said he had heard from Secretary Weinberger and said the Secretary was quite fond of me. So I had gotten some people moving and some ideas planted.

But most of all, I was mad. It had been ten weeks now, and the United States and the U.N. were on their knees, acting like whining children and helpless, hapless third-world countries. This was not right. This was not what Rich and I had sworn to give our lives for. I had no intention of standing for this level of inaction.

Beirut, April 21,
1988

Chapter 9

Dueling With
the Do-Nothings

Day 70
April 26, 1988

**The official American policy when hostages were taken
in the Middle East was to talk strongly and do nothing.
The lack of any substantial action by the U.S. or the U.N.
to free Rich made me focus my entire being on a single
goal: bring Rich safely home. My policy was exactly
the opposite of the bureaucrats: I would work behind
the scenes and do anything to get people in a position
of power to advance the cause of Rich's freedom.**

I planned to meet directly with top officials of the U.N. and the
Congress. I planned to go to Prince Bandar of Saudi Arabia, Rich's
former classmate; to Syrian President Hafez al-Assad; and even officials
in Algeria if I had to. Unlike Peggy Say, the vocal sister of hostage Terry
Anderson, I would not take my campaign public, but I would voice my
concern in any way I felt could be effective behind the scenes.

My work as a Marine Corps press officer gave me special access to high-level military and government officials, and I planned to exploit every advantage I had to bring him home.

As time went by, my personal circle of friends continued to shrink. I soon turned into a one-sided person. I felt like I had to be a one-man defender of Rich Higgins. My entire life revolved around my sole concern: bring Rich safely home. Everything I did or said was devoted to that goal. I dropped all other outside interests. I found myself spending time only with others who shared my single passion: my bubba group. Needless to say, any semblance of a normal social life dropped by the wayside, a casualty of more important things to do.

Rich's safe return became my obsession. I knew that many people who loved me might be offended — but that was a price I had to pay. One night in April I wrote to Rich in my journal:

> *I am fending off people who I know love me —*
> *like my family. I know I shouldn't and I do love them. But*
> *I have a small circle of trusted friends, and I don't want to*
> *expand it for fear I'll lose control. Everyone's got ideas,*
> *but I want to run the show with the trusted advice of the*
> *few I have let in to the circle. I know there are some people*
> *who need to be needed, need to be helpful, but I don't*
> *have enough to give to satisfy their needs.*

Other people weren't the only ones being hurt. As I read the newspaper and magazine stories, wire service articles, press releases, and intelligence reports every day, the names started appearing of the men who appeared to be directly involved in Rich's kidnapping. It also became clear who was working for Rich's release — and who was hindering the process. Before long, I found myself compiling a "friends and enemies" list. At the two-month mark, in the middle of April, I wrote in my journal:

> *What a terribly frustrating week. Sunday is two*
> *months. Only two months, but it seems like years. I keep*
> *thinking it may be years. And that'll be a lifetime. What*
> *will I do without you for a lifetime? There will be no life*
> *without you. I don't want a life without you. What has*
> *happened to you in these two months? Are you hurt? Are*
> *you sad? Are you mad? Are you strong? Please be strong*

*and brave and have lots of hope, because strength of body
and heart and mind will keep you safe and bring you home.*

*Are you in the Bekaa Valley? Some people think
you are now. And they say that is good, because that means
you are well. But that means you are well hidden, too.
Damn, I want you back. I'm afraid people are forgetting
to find you, to seek you, to get you back at all costs. I
don't want you to be forgotten, like the others. You are
not like the others. You were sent there to do a job, to
keep the peace. And they lost you and must get you back.
It is hard to be patient.*

*You're sleeping now, dreaming. Dream of me and
be happy. Dream of me loving you and be strong. Exercise
your body and your mind and come home to me tonight.*

I had two clocks in my head at all times — Eastern Daylight time
and Middle Eastern time. I knew at any moment what time it was where
Rich was. Every time I looked at my watch, I saw two times. I knew what
I was doing; I imagined what Rich might be doing.

I learned to scan huge amounts of information for news about
Rich. I learned to look for key words — "Higgins," "hostage." Even
years later, the shapes of the letters that made up these words jumped out
at me.

Major Michael Sullivan arrived in Washington from Lebanon in
mid-April. After consulting with officers in the various intelligence
services, including the Defense Intelligence Agency (DIA), Central
Intelligence Agency (CIA), State Department, and the Joint Chiefs of
Staff, he came to my home and brought me up to date on how Rich's
case was being handled in Lebanon. Mike and I talked throughout the
entire weekend. It was clear that he really admired Rich.

My Top Secret clearance gave me access to information that other
hostage relatives never saw, but the result was more often a curse than a
blessing. The inside information I was privy to usually turned out to be
vague and speculative and only increased my pain and needlessly
heightened my hopes. In my journal, I wrote to Rich:

I felt close to you today — I always do — but today felt different. Today I read a Secret SPECAT that said someone saw you. Wow! What did you look like? Where were you? Did you speak? Did you see that person? Were you sleeping? Were you OK? Were you bound? I have a million more questions, but they were unanswered.

☆☆☆

Day 65
April 21, 1988

The morning of April 21 arrived with no special signs or warnings. However, the buzz was that there was a picture of Rich and that Reuters had it. No one in the Defense Department seemed to be even interested in finding it. So I went to my friend, Charlie Aldinger of Reuters. Without any hesitation, he went to his cubbyhole to get on the phone and track down the photo for me. Within the hour he handed me a fuzzy black-and-white photo of a gaunt, slouched man in shapeless clothing staring down at the floor. The caption read, "Beirut, April 21, 1988. A copy of a photograph of U.S. Marine Colonel William Higgins delivered along with a statement by the Organization of the Oppressed in the World to a western news agency in West Beirut today. The group said it will put Higgins on trial for crimes he committed against the Lebanese and Palestinian people."

I rejoiced to see my husband, but he wasn't looking at me.

I took no time with the picture. Stoically and systematically I had copies made and passed them to my bubba group to pass on to those in the government who needed to see it. I was sure my government would analyze it, find out where he was, make sure he was alive, and get him out. Years later, I found out nothing was done.

Immediately after the release of this picture, I implemented my plan to talk with, convince, and hold accountable every person who was connected with Rich's well-being. On April 27, I went out with Laurette Gillespie, an old family friend and a college colleague of Rich's, to buy a "power suit" to wear the next week when I went to New York. There I had arranged to meet with Marrack Goulding, U.N. Undersecretary General for Special Political Affairs; Vernon A. Walters, U.S. Ambassador to the United Nations; and U.N. Secretary General Javier Perez de Cuellar.

I felt the need to talk with these powerful men face-to-face. I wanted them to know that they might not be answerable to the world for any inaction, but they were answerable to me. I knew that I had a lot of power at that moment, but I also knew from my work in Washington how transient power is. My power, I knew, might slip away at any moment. I wanted to use it while I still had it and hear what they were doing to bring Rich home. I knew that people in high places were apprehensive of me. They knew I was a Marine and that I couldn't be intimidated. They also knew that I was a professional press officer and couldn't easily be deceived or put off. They also knew I had immediate access to the press and could go to them in a heartbeat. I wanted to let these people know what I expected of them.

As a matter of protocol, I warned my Pentagon colleagues and superiors in advance of the meetings. In my office, no one batted an eye about my plans. In fact, all my colleagues thought it was great. Major General Gordie Fornell, then senior military assistant to the Secretary of Defense, said nothing. But when I called to talk to the Assistant Commandant of the Marine Corps, he called me back and gave me a big lecture about responsibility, perhaps to feel out whether I'd say anything against the Marine Corps or to see if I'd say or do anything that would bring ill-repute on the service. That was a disappointment. However, that was soon to become a rarity in the Marine Corps, once the senior leadership realized how circumspect I was.

Before I left for New York, I did what every seasoned communications professional does: prepare a list of talking points. When meeting with anyone whose time is limited, it is essential to have a clear, prioritized agenda. With these officials I wanted to cover three areas, and I didn't want to forget a thing.

The first item on my list was to establish my credibility face-to-face. I wanted them to see that I was not a hysterical woman, but rather a loyal wife, a patriotic citizen, and professional soldier with legitimate concerns seeking advice and guidance. I wanted them to know that in the two months since the kidnapping, my feelings had progressed from assurance that everyone was doing all that could be done to dissatisfaction. I wanted them to know that "quiet diplomacy" was not nearly good enough. And I wanted to emphasize that Rich was different from the American civilians who failed to heed the State Department's travel ban to Lebanon. He was not just another American pursuing his own agenda who got himself in trouble in a foreign land. Rich was an active-duty American military officer assigned under orders to perform official duties as commander of the United Nations Truce Supervisory Organization in Lebanon. As such, he was not a hostage. He was a prisoner of war.

Upon meeting Ambassador Goulding, I tried to impress this British long-time diplomat of my sincerity and goals. He was receptive and polite, but I never felt he was going to give an inch or ever really listen to me. It turned out that was true. He had his own agenda — for the good of U.N. peacekeeping in general and around the world. One peacekeeper, no matter how much Ambassador Goulding cared personally, was not going to influence his direction. And, unfortunately a little bit of Timor Goksell's message — that maybe Rich brought some of this on himself — seemed to find its way into his thinking, as far as I could tell.

I then met Ambassador Vernon Walters. Now this was a man! Vernon Anthony Walters retired from the Army in 1976 as a lieutenant general. In his distinguished Army career of thirty-five years, he had served as Staff Assistant to President Eisenhower and Interpreter to the President, Vice President, and high officials of the Department of State and the Department of Defense; Army Attache to Italy and Brazil; Defense Attache to France; and Acting Director and Deputy Director of the CIA. Powerful and larger than life, he was nonetheless a true patriot, warm and sincere, and someone with whom I could speak frankly.

As a result of my meeting with Ambassador Walters, he told Secretary of Defense Carlucci that he would speak about Rich's case with his old friend, Syrian President Hafez al-Assad. A few weeks later, he left for Syria to press the case for the release of the American hostages and Colonel Rich Higgins. I'd like to think that perhaps my talk with him made his mission more personal. Interestingly, it turned out Ambassador Walters was to be often at odds with our very own State Department in his quest to do what was right for a fellow military officer.

I was ushered into the U.N. Secretary General Javier Perez de Cuellar's office along with a wave of press and photographers. They had obviously gone through this drill before. The press asked no questions; the photographers' bulbs popped endlessly. The Secretary General and I stood at his couch, then sat, shaking hands and mumbling niceties. However, I began to panic that we wouldn't have any time in private to speak openly.

Then as quickly as they flowed in, the press flowed out, the door shut, and we were alone. He was a soft-spoken gentleman, whose eyes you could look into. He seemed to listen when I spoke and seemed sincere in wanting to help. However, I was to find out that these very powerful men at the top just can't do what they want to do. They listen to their advisors who are less likely to be influenced by emotions and passions, those emotions and passions which sometimes cause one to do the right thing, not necessarily the politic thing.

At the end of each meeting with the United Nations officials, I left each a list of twenty-six questions. Each question was designed to determine how to get Rich back home quickly and safely. It was designed to be bold but not disrespectful. I told each of the men that I knew they couldn't answer each of them, but that by studying and circulating the list, they might help ensure that all the questions eventually got asked — and even answered.

26 Questions For The United Nations:

1. Who has ultimate responsibility to secure Colonel Higgins' release?

2. What has the U.N. done to secure his release?

3. Who within the U.N. has ultimate responsibility for gaining Colonel Higgins' release?

4. Why has the U.N. thus far been unsuccessful in securing his release?

5. What is the principal problem in getting his release?

6. Who has responsibility to solve that problem?

7. Do we have any firm knowledge of what group and what person within that group has control of him?

8. What do the people who have control of him really want in return for his release?

9. Who can give that to them?

10. Is anybody in communication with them?

11. Is there anybody who can be in communication with them who is not now communicating with them?

12. Has anyone communicated with Iran the seriousness of this action and of their complicity in it? Who? How?

13. Has the U.N. communicated with the Iranian permanent representative about this? What is his response?

14. Are there any restrictions on my travel and what are they?

15. To whom can I write? To whom can I talk? With whom can I visit? In the Arab world or elsewhere? Public officials? Country representatives? Private citizens, either U.S. or other?

16. Who can help free him?

17. Has anyone considered using the PLO as an intermediary? Has the U.N. communicated with the PLO?

18. Do we know who in Syria, Lebanon, Iran, or Algeria — public or private — can help free him?

19. Have they been contacted?

20. By whom?

21. Are other countries helping us? How?

22. How can we use the media? Communication with the kidnappers? Disinformation? Public support?

23. Would it be useful to write a piece for a major paper in Lebanon, such as An Nahar?

24. Has the U.N. considered, and/or taken the issue up with the countries in the region, that the U.S. may withdraw from funding of UNIFIL and staffing of UNTSO/OGL?

25. How and where can we push the system? Who is not doing something they can be doing?

26. Is everything that can be done being done?

My first meeting with a high-level elected U.S. government official took place in late April 1988, after my meetings with the U.N. officials. My choice of officials with whom to meet was governed solely by two factors: who seemed to be in a position to help, and of those, who would meet with me. On the Republican side of the aisle, I found support and encouragement from a number of senators, including Senators Bob Dole, John Warner, John McCain, Mitch McConnell, and Nancy Kassebaum.

Unfortunately, few Democrats would speak with me. Senate Majority Leader George Mitchell wouldn't see me. I saw this as a totally non-partisan issue. I was dismayed to learn that it wasn't so and sadly realized everything in Washington is partisan. How foolish of me not to have known that.

The first senator to talk with me was John W. Warner (R-Virginia). I visited him at his office on Capitol Hill, just after I spoke with the U.N. officials. I covered the same agenda, the same way, and left the same questions. I was to find lots of sympathy and varying degrees of sincerity in this and subsequent congressional visits. But there was no staying power; I found no sponsor who was willing to put this on the top of his agenda and keep it there. While I thought I was accomplishing something by becoming admired by these men, it turns out that it may have been just chivalrous patronization on many of their parts.

Brassy as it might have seemed, the direct approach seemed to work. I think I accomplished my first goal: to impress them with my calm, deliberate, respectful demeanor. In the halls of power, women are not always respected. I wanted to show them I was not a hysterical woman, but a force to be reckoned with. I think I accomplished that. Senator Warner called Ambassador Walters to say he had met me, "an articulate young woman," and Ambassador Walters set up and held a meeting with Secretary of Defense Frank Carlucci, during which Mr. Carlucci said they talked about me and Rich's case.

I felt some sense that the U.N. was convinced that obtaining Rich's freedom was their responsibility. They seemed to be pursuing a solution along several tracks, and I believed it was possible that one of them might work.

Nevertheless, I still had two specific goals. The first was to achieve more recognition from the U.S. government that Rich was not just one of the hostages, but an active duty military man working under the orders of the U.S. government to assist the United Nations.

The second goal was to see an interagency task force formed which would include representatives from the Marine Corps, Department of State, Department of Defense, National Security Council, Congress, and the United Nations. Its role would be to closely and constantly monitor all angles of the situation and share information.

The last step after my rounds of talks with high-level officials was done to mend any fences I may have inadvertently trampled with the Marine Corps. I visited the Marine Corps Chief of Staff. I thought that the Corps might have felt that they'd had their toes stepped on by a disgruntled Marine who thought that her needs were not being met by the chain of command. I wanted to tell the Corps that this was not the case, that I had kept my chain of command informed, that the Corps had been very supportive, and that I was using the access I had at the levels and in the places I felt it could best be applied. I think they came to understand this, and I had very little trouble in the future worrying about burning any Marine bridges.

May arrived, the third new month since Rich's capture. That was the month that Rich's personal effects were shipped back to me. How I wished that Timor Goksell and Daniel Schorr had been there when the crate was unpacked. Maybe if they had been able to touch Rich's wallet or see what he had in his dresser drawers the day he was kidnapped they could get some sense of him, the man they had both maligned — and endangered.

Then I saw a message from the State Department to Ambassador Walters, telling him not to interfere with the Syrians or to discuss the Amal/Hezbollah fighting. For me, that translated directly into: Don't do anything to get Rich out. What is their strategy? What are they trying to do?

My boss, Dan Howard, said he talked to Ambassador Bremer's office at the State Department. State was angry that I had dared to talk directly with Ambassador Walters. Mr. Howard told Bremer that I had gone up to talk with Undersecretary Goulding at the United Nations and that Ambassador Walters had asked to speak with me, not the other way around, which was true. Where was the outrage that Rich was being held prisoner by fanatical lunatics? God knows, it wasn't at the State Department. They only seemed to be concerned with protocol.

I didn't want Rich to worry about the flame of hope being snuffed out at this end of the world. That worry was my job to shoulder. The next day I went to talk with Ambassador Bremer myself. After reading and appreciating his article on prisoners of war and counter-terrorism, I had hoped my fears were unfounded. I had hoped something would happen before the meeting to restore my faith in our government — specifically the State Department — because I didn't want to lose my temper. I couldn't help but think that we missed a window of opportunity while Ambassador Walters was in Syria — with a State Department gag in his mouth. I thought to myself, God knows how we get anything done in this country.

☆☆☆

Day 100

May 26, 1988

This morning, like every morning, my mind was on Rich. I was living each day intensely, focused. There was little in the message traffic of interest to me. Then another of the emotional roller-coaster cycles started. I had lunch with Ty Tisdale and Bruce Mackey, Army officers who were Middle Eastern specialists and had both known Rich. Tisdale gave me a short briefing over lunch. He was most pessimistic of all about depending on the Shi'ites to find and free Rich. He said only two things have ever freed hostages — concessions or physical harm — neither of which the U.S. was prepared to use.

This added another layer of gloom on my growing feelings of depression, so I threw myself into my work. Then Fred Francis, NBC's Pentagon correspondent (who, second only to my friends at the Defense Intelligence Agency, gave me the best news scoops I got) came in and told me the best news yet: A team of U.S. journalists was being called to Damascus secretly. They were told they were going to Beirut, where they would "see some surprises." This was to be about midnight that night. He said he knew there had been a political deal and felt that meant hostages. I couldn't help but be excited, but it could have meant anything — including any other hostages besides Rich.

On the one hand, I couldn't imagine it happening; on the other — why not? OK, I reasoned, if it's to be midnight here, that's 6 A.M. for Rich. If it were true, I tried to imagine how he would be affected. Would they let him sleep tonight? Would they make him shave and get cleaned up? Would they move him? Would they tell him? I didn't want to think about those things, because I'd been let down so many times before, but hope springs eternal in the breast of every hostage family member.

The next evening, I again wrote to Rich:

> *I'm writing you early tonight — it's only 8 P.M.*
> *That means it's 2 A.M. where you are. Where are you? If*
> *you're in Beirut, you might be awake. The Syrians went in*
> *today. It was a day we've all been waiting for, but I don't*
> *think the desired effect will happen. They invited a large*
> *news team in with them and said, 'There will be surprises,'*
> *but so far, no surprises except some remarkable shots of*
> *war-torn south Beirut and a close-up of one of the Hamadi*
> *brothers.[18] That's not a good enough surprise for me.*

That morning I had heard a disturbing story. An Iranian plane was at Beirut Airport earlier in the week and supposedly took Rich and two other hostages to Tehran. I knew it sounded far-fetched, but during the course of the day I put a scenario together that sounded very plausible. Fred Francis, Ty Tisdale, and Bruce Mackey all agreed it was plausible. Syria wants to look good and to stay friends with Iran. They want to be the heroes and release the hostages, yet Iran wants to keep at least some

---

[18] Muhammad Ali Hamadi, one of a notorious family of terrorists, was implicated in the hijacking of TWA Flight 847, captured and imprisoned in Germany.

of them (Rich, Terry Anderson, Tom Sutherland, I surmised). The others have become liabilities. So they make a deal — Syria looks the other way at the airport, Iran spirits out three men, and Syria comes into the suburbs and jointly Iran and Syria free the hostages — except they can't find three of them. That's the scenario which came to my mind.

I wrote to Rich, *I don't know how it's going to end because unless they free all or prove there are no more, then they're not really heroes. But it sounds like the best arrangement to me. God, I hope it's not true.* Three days later, after meeting with State Department officials and gathering more news reports, I found out that this scenario — like so many other scraps of hope — never had any substance.

That night, before I went to bed, I wrote to Rich: *I'm very sad and lonely tonight. I hope you aren't — be strong, my love, be a warrior. When this is over I'll make you soften. But now be hard and tough.*

In better times
January 1988
The Sinai

Chapter 10
Eight Hostages and a POW

In Washington, spring started to turn into summer, but the change of seasons was lost on me. It was now three months since the terrorists had pulled Rich from his muddy Jeep. In those twelve weeks, neither the United States nor the United Nations had taken any real responsibility for obtaining his safe return.

The Hezbollah and Amal factions were at each other's throats, the worst fighting in five years. Every time they clashed, my bubba group and I held a conference. What did it mean? Would it hurt or help Rich's chances for release? What could we do? What should I think? What should I tell the family?

The French hostages were released yesterday. Everyone is up in arms because they believe France paid a big ransom. I hear they have expelled a certain Iranian, intend to moderate their relations with Iran, have released a loan payment from the Shah's regime, and paid a sum

(I hear as "low" as $5 million) for "room and board" for three years. Pretty good digs, huh? What is your hotel worth? Now these Frenchmen are saying the American hostages have been beaten. I don't believe you're with those guys, but I also don't disbelieve that you may have been beaten. I'll get you back and take care of you however you are — I love you however I get you back...

After the weekend, I felt strongly that your release would be any day now, just a couple of weeks, but as hour by hour and day by day passes by, I get more discouraged. Things are happening though. I see more message traffic; people are beginning to talk. Ambassador Walters is on our side and is traveling. Good things are happening, but I'm just strung out — I can't keep my mind on anything but you. At work and at home, I'm good only at short-term projects.

There are favorable things happening with efforts to negotiate an end to the Amal and Hezbollah infighting. Fadlallah[19] is calling for the Hezbollah to release their hostages by May 17, the end of Ramadan. Oh, I hope it's you! That would be a great date to have you back. It all seems so plausible, so reasonable, so right. I tell myself I can't get my hopes up, but I can't help it, I'm so in love with you.

By the end of the third month after Rich's abduction, I had formulated two specific goals: get the U.S. government to identify and treat Rich as a military prisoner of war, not as a civilian hostage, and get the United Nations to publicly condemn the kidnapping and take responsibility for obtaining Rich's safe return.

As far as I was concerned, the U.N. was a major obstacle to obtaining Rich's release. They were forever vague, equivocal, and ambivalent about Rich's status, their responsibility, and how to get him back. One day they'd be optimistic about his release; the next, they'd suggest that there was nothing they could do. The third day, they'd say

---

[19] Sheikh Muhammad Hussein Fadlallah, the spiritual leader of Hezbollah, generally conceded to be one of its main leaders.

Rich would be released before the other hostages. It drove me crazy. Every day I wrestled with the emotional implications of the U.N.'s latest vacillating position.

Within our own government, no one took up his cause, led the charge, became involved in proactive efforts to free Rich, or wanted to take charge of getting him back. Many paid lip service to his predicament; few attempted to do anything. Republican leaders generally supported my positions and efforts; Democratic leaders refused to get involved.

My bubba group and I felt that the U.S. government's best approach would be to form an interagency task force to coordinate all efforts that could help bring about Rich's release. We felt it should consist of representatives from the Marine Corps, Department of State, Department of Defense, National Security Council, National Security Commission, and Congress. I could never convince anyone to form the work group.

U.N. Ambassador Vernon A. Walters turned out to be Rich's best friend and ally within our government. Walters had real contacts with the Syrians and other Middle East officials. He was the only high-level State Department official who was willing to buck the system and make special mention of Rich during his overseas visits and talks with foreign officials.

As the weeks turned into months, with no sign of Rich's imminent release, I found myself turning progressively more inward. Anything but short, superficial contact with friends and relatives became less and less frequent. My contacts with the outside world diminished. I withdrew further and further into my own shell, which was the only place I could be sure I was still in control of some part of my personal life.

From that quiet, still place inside myself, I sought the answers to the unanswerable questions. Why had this happened? Why Rich? Why me? How long will it last? Will he come back safely? Will he come back at all? The result of that introspection was an essay I wrote to help me deal with the issues I was confronting and express some of the emotions I was hiding. It was published in the *Marine Corps Gazette*.

Honor, Courage, and Good Sense —

A Shield for Survival
An essay by Robin L. Higgins

Of late, I have been seeking the answers to questions of survival and solace at a very personal level. How do I survive? How do I help my husband survive? The second question is easy to answer, hard to live with — I can't. In those two words alone, I find great discomfort. But I must overcome that feeling and find a way to survive, and through that quest, I must have faith that Rich, too, is traveling a similar path. I am here, surrounded by the familiarity of family, friends, books, my country and Corps. It is my duty to survive, to commune with Rich, and to sustain him, because he is alone.

In my quest to survive, certain words keep returning to my mind, words which Rich and I have shared, and somehow they give me strength. "Honor," "courage," and "good sense" are words which, to us who are Marines, have always packed much meaning, words which have new, inspirational, intense meaning now. It's uncanny what depth of feeling a mere word can evoke, what comfort a sound can provide, what satisfaction a few pen strokes can bear.

I have some quotes of Winston Churchill's on yellow notes on my wall over my desk at the office. As I work and receive signals which distract me from my work, I read them, think of them, mull over their meaning. I think of the man who first uttered these words — and just what made him put his thoughts into these precise words, and I think of the men and women who have taken strength and solace from the words since they were written. Let me share them with you:

Honor — "The only guide to a man is his conscience; the only shield to his memory is the rectitude and sincerity of his actions. It is very imprudent to walk through life without this shield, because we are so often mocked by the failure of our hopes and the upsetting of our calculations; but with this shield, however the fates may play, we march always in the ranks of honor."

Courage — "True courage swims against the tide. True courage begins when everyone else has either given in or stopped fighting. True courage is never being swept along by what everyone else is doing. True courage is often lonely. On our journey I pray that we will have as our companions Faith to light the road ahead, for dark is the path of the nation that walks without faith; Enthusiasm that has made us great and will keep us a force for good in the world; and finally Courage, greatest of all human virtues since it guarantees all of the others."

Good sense — "Never give in, never give in, never, never, never in nothing great or small, large or petty — never give in except to convictions of honor and good sense."

Like faith in God, I have come to have faith in these words. I believe there is a fabric that weaves people of conscience through the ages and around the world. That fabric is bound with words — words of strong, smart men and women, such as those whose quotations hang on my wall. Those words represent the "moral and spiritual lineage" of men and women of honor, courage, and good sense. Bound into this fabric are the lives and loves of soldiers and their families from all times, those who came home and those who didn't, and those whose fate remains unknown.[20] Rich's life is woven on the edge of that fabric

[20] John William Gardner, *Morale*, W.W. Norton Co., New York, March 1980, p. 47.

now. His unshakable devotion to honor, his undeniable courage, and his abiding good sense shield him from harm — and the rich tapestry embraces me. "Remember them that are in bonds, as bound with them; and them which suffer adversity, as being yourselves also in the body." (Hebrews 13:3). This is my shield.

Because of my desire to retain my privacy and devote all my energy to obtaining Rich's safe return, I deliberately distanced myself from the other hostage families. I especially avoided contact with their vocal spokeswoman, Peggy Say, sister of hostage Terry Anderson. She was strident in denouncing the inaction on the part of the U.S. government. That was not my style. I preferred to take the high road, maintain my dignity and work quietly behind the scenes.

Say was as driven to obtain the release of her brother as I was to see Rich freed, yet she and I were as different as night and day. She was public, outspoken, and vocal; I was private, reserved, and restrained. I never knew whether she sought the mantle of spokeswoman for the other hostage families or whether she assumed it at the request of the families themselves.

Sometimes I shuddered at her caustic comments and wondered if she wasn't using the hostage families as a springboard to vault herself into the limelight. Other times I wondered if my own lack of visibility was hurting Rich's chances for freedom. In the nebulous world of hostage-taking, there was no way to tell what would work and what would hurt. On May 13 I wrote to Rich:

> *Today they had a ceremony at Arlington for CIA station chief William Buckley. Luckily, no one told me about it beforehand, because I would've wanted to be there. Peggy Say and the "No Greater Love" organization of hostage families were there. She spoke, and the hostage families were featured. To me, it looks like their grief is being exploited, and I won't be a party to it. It's sad, though. I do feel a bond with the other hostage families — but I feel a closer bond with the families of POWs. They have known the agony of sending a man to war and waiting for him. Those are the ones I feel closest to. And*

with those who have suffered in silence, not those who
have gone on television, who have cried in groups. I do
not want to get friendly with other hostage families. I am
a private person — thrust into a very public role — and I
will not make it more public than I have to. My goal is to
love you and to bring you home. Nothing else. My grief is
for you and with you alone.

In early July, a feature story about the Lebanon hostage families appeared in *People* magazine. I repeatedly declined to be interviewed, even though they contacted me and the family numerous times to say we were the only ones not participating. I was particularly irked that a reporter contacted Uncle Delbert asking him if the stress was "pulling the family apart." Delbert Eagle was Rich's favorite uncle — and Richard was his favorite nephew. Delbert was an erudite, popular circuit judge in Lancaster, Kentucky, now in his late 80s. I found that to be a particularly indelicate question to ask of this frail, old man.

In the article, some of the families spoke against the government; some remained apolitical. The report stated that, on the one hand, I won't give interviews, and on the other, Peggy Say works "tirelessly" for her brother's release, lobbies Congress, and the like. It made it sound as if by my not giving interviews — *ergo*, I was doing nothing for Rich's release. Of course, the truth is that just about everybody who counted in Washington had me on their phone or in their office, lobbying privately for Rich's return. Public media interviews had given Peggy Say high visibility — but I was convinced that my choice of quiet diplomacy and behind-the-scenes contacts was better for Rich. It hurt to read the insinuations, but I would not allow myself to respond.

I'll never know if my private demands benefitted or hurt Rich's cause. In the *People* magazine case, I thought at the time that my lack of participation could be interpreted by his captors as "See, he must really be a spy. Even his family won't speak." Nevertheless, I didn't want to talk to the writers. I was afraid of being exploited and terrified that any statements I might give would be misinterpreted or twisted.

A few weeks later, I visited the State Department, where I was shown a weak-kneed State Department cable to the U.N. asking that they condemn all kidnapping. Only four months after the kidnapping, and already it was getting harder for me to believe differently from what Peggy Say was saying: that all the hostages had been abandoned by their government.

I vowed to make a visit to see Secretary of Defense Carlucci. He had known Rich personally, having been Deputy Secretary of Defense while Rich was working for his predecessor, Caspar Weinberger. I requested the visit and carefully prepared and prioritized my talking points. He saw me a few days later.

I told the Secretary that I was getting the runaround from all levels of the federal government. I told him that for four months, I had talked to people within the system in all agencies of government. I gave people my written list of questions and got lots of patronizing smiles and wringing of hands — but no answers or action. I told him that I was now firmly convinced that the government was not doing anything to secure Rich's release. In fact, I believed that in some cases, the State Department was even opposing some efforts.

The State Department would not take any actions which they believed would highlight Rich's importance. I don't know if they truly believed this would be bad for Rich or if they believed it would cast them in a bad light with Peggy Say and the others. Anyway they were so firmly convinced of this course of action — or rather, inaction — that they had convinced the U.N. that he was not important. They tried to keep Ambassador Walters from bringing up Rich's case with Syrian President Hafez el-Assad.

On one hand the State Department was downplaying Rich's importance; on the other hand, I told Mr. Carlucci, they kept telling me that the U.N. connection was Rich's best hope.

I told the Secretary that the U.S. was not acting — only reacting. I asked him why we couldn't make the first move. The State Department claimed that direct action would only justify to Hezbollah their own importance. That concept was a farce. Hezbollah was indeed important. By hiding the truth, we were not fooling Hezbollah or the Iranians — only the American people. I asked him why we couldn't ask them what they want in return for the hostages. We might find that their demands weren't all that unrealistic. Maybe they would have been.

But until we asked, they would never tell us. That was one root of the hostage stalemate.

I told him I felt that Peggy Say was wrong to publicly criticize the American government. I told him that I thought it best to work quietly, not because I cared about myself, my career, or the government, but because I was firmly convinced that my public criticism could be harmful to Rich.

The Secretary listened attentively as I made my case. I closed with three questions. The first was, "Is my assessment of the do-nothing stance of our government correct, or are we, in fact, doing something to obtain Rich's freedom?" Then, "Has the Defense Department made known its true concern about this military man, and what are our actions? Is this the right moral signal to send to our people in uniform?" Finally, I asked him, "What else can I do?" I told him that I intended to speak with the Commandant of the Marine Corps and every senator and congressman who would listen.

Mr. Carlucci listened to me speak for a full half-hour. He agreed with me on all points. He agreed that the State Department was erratic in its policy. He said that he'd talk to Secretary of State George Schultz again, but then cautioned me. He agreed with me that Rich was "one of their own," but warned that in Washington, if you push too hard for one of your own (as the CIA had for their station chief, William Buckley), "people become suspicious of your motives." I had to agree with him — but it made me sick to think that this was the way America made foreign policy decisions. That night I wrote to Rich in my journal, *I still don't have you, but the Secretary of Defense listened to me, I made my points, and he promised to talk to the Secretary of State. Perhaps we'll make headway.*

After I left the Secretary's office, I vowed to redouble my efforts to bring about change in how Rich's case was being handled. On the first of June I put together a fact sheet which I subsequently distributed to every group and individual I felt could help. I gave them the following guidance:

1. Colonel Higgins is different from other hostages and should not be dealt with in the same context. Higgins was in the right place, at the right time, doing a job assigned him by the U.S. government and the U.N. Others were

warned to get out of Lebanon. In effect, Higgins is a POW whose release should be sought as actively as previous POWs.

2. U.N. and State Department should be aggressive, not simply responsive, in their attempts to get Higgins released. They should be proactive rather than reactive. They should have a strategy, not just a policy ("We don't negotiate with terrorists.").

3. U.N. and State should be working with other countries which have better relations with Iran than does the United States. France, Algeria, and Syria are good prospects. Government and private individuals in these countries and others must be identified and pressured to assist.

4. U.S. must express its outrage at the United Nations and threaten further cuts in funding unless more is done (or conversely, paying what has been withheld if something is done). U.N. should consider sanctions against Lebanon, hitting the people where it hurts until adequate and appropriate pressure is leveled against those responsible.

5. Overall guidance: Work privately and confidentially within the system. Colonel Higgins' cause is not well served by publicity and/or overt criticism of the U.S. government.

In June 1988 I publicly raised the issue of whether Rich was a hostage — as the U.N. and the U.S. government were categorizing him — or a prisoner of war (POW) under the Geneva Convention. I believed that there were strong grounds to argue that he was a prisoner of war.

Officially, Rich was carried in the Marine Corps rolls as "missing" with a subcategory of "detained in a foreign country against his will." Unlike the other eight Americans being held captive in Lebanon, Rich had been sent there under orders from the U.S. government. The others had gone to Lebanon of their own free will and remained there despite demands by the State Department that they leave.

I never felt even for a moment that the other hostages were less deserving of the government's efforts than was Rich. All were being held captive against their will in a foreign land. Their agony and that of their families was no less overwhelming than mine.

But Rich was not a hostage, for a hostage is a hapless civilian trapped by fate in the line of fire and held for some sick political or financial reason. No, he was a prisoner of war: a serviceman on active duty, doing what he was ordered to do by his country, and captured because he was an official representative of his country and its policies.

When servicemen or women are captured, they are required by the Uniform Code of Military Justice to behave as prisoners of war, not hostages. They live each day by the Code of Conduct which states: *I am an American, fighting in the Armed Forces which guard my country and our way of life. I am prepared to give my life in their defense... I will never forget that I am an American, fighting for freedom, responsible for my actions, and dedicated to the principles which made my country free. I will trust in my God and in the United States of America.*

Under the Geneva Convention and international law, those who hold POWs are required to furnish the prisoners humane treatment, medical care, and access to the International Red Cross. Political hostages receive no such rights.

Because neither the U.S. nor the U.N. wanted to give legitimacy to the terrorists, they never acknowledged the Hezbollah, never placed special pressure or demands on them, nor did they place any sanctions on them or anyone else.

Within the U.S. government, the State Department, not the Defense Department, had the lead. That meant that Rich's case would be pursued through diplomacy, not military might. There were no signs that the U.S. would resort to retribution, retaliation, or rescue. I knew that if they had the opportunity, a battalion of Marines was ready and would have jumped at the chance to rescue Rich — but they never got the call to go. It is no wonder that the terrorists had no fear of the U.S. government.

Servicemen and women wear the uniform of this country and leave their families behind to fight for this country because they believe this country will come after them when they fall. In Rich's case, the U.S. government seemed willing to break this sacred pledge.

I found a kindred spirit in a book I read — a woman walking an eerily similar path in an earlier time. *In Love and War*, by Jim and Sybil Stockdale about Jim's eight years in a North Vietnamese prison, stopped me in my tracks.

I first picked up the book to try to help me answer some questions: How would Rich — who was, after all, a trained military officer like Jim Stockdale was — react? What would give him strength? I knew he had read and studied and learned much from the accounts of Vietnam's POWs. He may have even read this exact book. And how would I cope? What would give me strength? Was there something that others — like Sybil, who was, after all, just an ordinary, loving wife like I was — had done before me that I could learn from? I was to learn from every turn of every page just how similar our paths were.

In the beginning, I learned that Jim Stockdale was then a Navy commander (the same rank as Rich), a good and professional officer who knew the risks, but was dedicated to his mission, to his service, and to his country. Same as Rich. Small, personal similarities continued to reel me in to those pages: Sybil remembered when Jim came home for emergency leave to visit his father who was seriously ill ("I felt guilty about being so excited at the prospect of seeing Jim, with his dad's illness the cause. But a visit seemed like a gift from God — we'd been separated for more than four months."). Rich, too, came home for emergency leave for the same reason, also after about four months. I felt the same mix of elation and guilt. I learned Jim Stockdale's birthday was the same as mine — two days before Christmas. We were them, and they were us.

When she learned Jim was missing, Sybil said, "No tears gushed forth. No screams of anguish. Just a puzzling sensation of shock that this was happening to me." As she methodically worked to gain control of her life and that of her family, while tirelessly persevering against odds to bring him home, she found she heard him reminding her of his favorite little axioms, "Always try to turn a disadvantage into an advantage." Rich had a similar one that kept resounding in my mind: "Every problem is an opportunity."

Sybil found herself going into meetings with high-level government officials, whispering to herself: "Maybe if he thought I was a thoughtful person, he'd try even harder to do whatever he could to help Jim." She knew she had to be careful "not to become shrill or too emotional" or she'd be "written off as an unbalanced female." I, too, instinctively, steeled myself in the same way. Sybil found herself keeping two times in her head, the time where she was and the time where he was. I was doing the same!

All the while, in a dark, dank Vietnamese prison, Jim was being tortured and denigrated in the worst ways. While his body was wracked with pain, his mind was crazy with hopelessness and despair. But he never gave up because he was a patriot and a husband; love of his country and his wife kept him going. He, too, manipulated his mind into surviving. So, too, I knew every day that Rich did.

Sybil had an almost identical problem with the State Department. The military prisoners had been given a low priority. The principle was that they were not prisoners, but "hostages," in this case saying that "the communists would demand a quid pro quo for treating them [the POWs] decently and that they [the U.S. government] had no intention of granting any concessions." Although I conceded the civilians held in Lebanon were indeed hostages, Colonel Higgins was not — he was a military man, ordered to be there, and was therefore a prisoner of war. I never could get anyone in the government to agree with me. Sybil's faith that her government would "do the right thing" wavered, and so did mine. Although the government officials she met were long since replaced by others, they had the very same "detached, casual attitudes."

☆☆☆

Day 118
June 13, 1988

All the time that the hostage crisis was going on, I was still trying to be a good stepmom to Chrissy. I felt I was failing at that. But this was the day she graduated from high school. This was the day that Rich was supposed to be back for. That night, I wrote to Rich:

Yesterday was baccalaureate. It was fun to see Chrissy in her cap and gown going around with her friends (she's not the solemn type). She is wild...but she is cute and seems to be a happy kid despite what's going on in her head. In fact, last night for the first time she woke me up at 2:30 A.M. crying that she had a bad dream that you had been killed. I hugged her and told her it was a dream, that you were going to be fine, and she went to bed shortly after that. Last night was the maddest I have been at those bastards who have you — how dare they ruin this graduation week for Chrissy. She tries to put on a brave front and usually does well, but she's just a kid inside.

Today I made a decision to take some time off. I feel I need it really badly. I haven't taken any time since February 17 and I'm getting stressed out. I feel like I'm leaving you — but friends say I'm taking you with me, and that makes it seem better. After graduation I'm going to head up to West Virginia, to the mountains to a spa. For three days I will hike, run, swim, read, sit in the whirlpool, and think of you. It won't be fun — it'll be very lonely — but maybe I can get rid of some of this stress; maybe something will happen while I'm out of the Pentagon. How are your days? Are you finding thoughts and things to keep you busy? Maybe by going through my days in your head, it'll make time pass faster for you.

My next goal was the U.N. resolution condemning Rich's kidnapping and demanding his return. My relationship with the United Nations typified the Kafkaesque world I was living in during the first summer after his abduction. On the one hand, I held the U.N. responsible for obtaining his safe return. To ensure that they had no excuse for considering me a problem to be dealt with, I had to avoid saying or doing anything in public that would jeopardize my relationship with them. On the other hand, I was furious at their cavalier disregard for Rich's good name and for the massive passivity they showed when it came time for anything beyond mouthing hollow platitudes. As a result, I constantly felt the need to stifle my anger and rein in my natural instincts to goad them into action through public criticism.

I longed to publicly call them to task for their spineless ineptitude, but I knew that to do so would give them an excuse to ignore the pursuit of Rich's safe return. As a result, I had to swallow my pride, pretend I respected them, and cajole, suggest, and plead with them to do a tenth of what they should have been doing without urging. For a Marine Corps officer accustomed to taking charge and getting jobs done, I found the paralysis this situation shackled me with was excruciating, and it ate at me.

It was during one of the brainstorming sessions with my bubbas that we came up with the idea of a U.N. resolution. My suggesting this would once and for all make the U.N. put up or shut up — that is, to be forced to claim the responsibility out loud that they claimed to me in private. They wouldn't then be able to do nothing; they would have to do something. All member nations would have to abide by the resolution. And the situation would be elevated to where it belonged. At least, this is what I thought.

When I suggested it to Marrack Goulding at the U.N., he downplayed the need for such a resolution and expressed some inability to make such a resolution pass. He explained how difficult it was to get the Security Council all to agree to anything, no less something like this (as minuscule as this, is what I thought I heard him saying between his lines of measured speech).

However, when he carried the message to others in the halls of the U.N., someone must have liked the idea, because in subsequent phone conversations with him, he always brought up the progress of the resolution. I saw the resolution referred to in several State Department messages. Naturally, the State Department thought the resolution should refer to all hostages, not just Colonel Higgins. They backed down from that. That wouldn't have any meaning at all.

The resolution seemed to take on a life of its own, and one day Mr. Goulding called me to say it was going to happen.

When July 29 arrived, it turned out to be a wonderful day — for the most part. I was in New York at the U.N., where I met with Ambassador Goulding alone. He gave me a thorough briefing about his recent trip to the Mideast. The big problem, he revealed, was the statement he passed on from Nabih Berri, Lebanon's Minister of Justice. Soon after Rich's capture, Berri said he and Amal had become convinced that Rich was indeed a spy. They deduced this, he said, from Rich's connection to Secretary Weinberger and President Reagan's off-the-cuff statement that "they won't get any secrets out of him." Berri said that's when the Amal stopped searching. Berri said that everyone in the Arab world believed that.

Next, I walked to Secretary General de Cuellar's office. I walked in the door to shake his hand. He motioned me to sit down — and the same sea of photographers I remembered from my last visit rolled in behind us. The Secretary General had just been chosen as ABC's person of the week. Amidst the crowd, I found myself once again wondering if we were going to get to talk without all those people around. But after a few minutes, like clockwork, they were ushered out, and we got down to talking.

The Secretary had just met with Iran's foreign minister, Ali Akbar Velayati, and informed me that he had told Velayati in no uncertain terms that he wanted "his man, Colonel Higgins back." Mr. Velayati said he'd do what he could when he returned to Iran. De Cuellar said, "No, now." He said, "As a special favor to me, give me back Higgins." I was impressed. According to the Secretary General, the Iranian didn't say no.

Suddenly we were walking down echoing halls to the Security Council. These were the very halls and the very Council chambers I visited years ago as a Long Island elementary school girl on field trips. Here I was, and the press was in one location, snapping pictures of me and asking me to speak with them. I stood very, very tall, smiled as proudly as I could, and nodded politely.

At the 2,822nd meeting of the U.N. Security Council, I heard a small voice in a monotonous tone reading the resolution, the first resolution, I was later told, in honor of a single person since the passing of U Thant, the U.N.'s Secretary General.

Resolution #618

Taking note of paragraph 23 of the Secretary-General's report on the United Nations Interim Force in Lebanon (UNIFIL) (S/20053), concerning the abduction of Lieutenant-Colonel William Richard Higgins, a military observer of the United Nations Truce Supervision Organization serving with the United Nations Interim Force in Lebanon,

Recalling the Secretary-General's special report on the United Nations Interim Force in Lebanon (S/19617),

Recalling also its resolution 579 (1985), which, *inter alia*, condemned unequivocally all acts of hostage-taking and abduction and called for the immediate release of all hostages and abducted persons wherever and by whomever they are being held,

Condemns the abduction of Lieutenant Colonel Higgins;

1. Demands his immediate release;

2. Calls upon Member States to use their influence in any way possible to promote the implementation of this resolution.

   After that, I never heard much about U.N. Security Council Resolution #618.

The seven U.S. Marine Corps officers
Assigned to UNTSO, South Lebanon, 1987
(Front row) Ron Johnson, George Solly, Steve Piccirelli
(Back row) Jim Walsh, Mike Sullivan, Frank Hart, and Rich

Chapter 11

A Disillusioned Patriot

Day 167
August 1, 1988

When the United Nations adopted Resolution #618, U.N. officials emphasized the fact that Rich was only the second individual ever to have a resolution passed on his behalf. At the announcement, reporters and television crews were there to see the U.N. praised for their humanitarian efforts. They had, after all, done their job. Top officials had convened, discussed, and decided to denounce the injustice of holding a U.N. man hostage.

But after media attention faded and Rich became old news again, the resolution was rarely mentioned. Like almost every official action taken on Rich's behalf, it had been lip service. Despite the fanfare and swarms of television cameras, Resolution #618 was just as meaningless as the efforts I'd seen from our own government.

Both the U.N. and the U.S. felt that all they could do was ask for Rich's return. The government sent diplomatic memos saying that they condemned the kidnapping, and then the U.N. passed a resolution with Rich's name attached. As far as they were concerned, they had done all they could. They thought their job was done, but they were wrong. Until Rich was home, their job would never be done.

As soon as the Hezbollah heard about Resolution #618, they rejected it, calling it a plot against the Muslims and mujahadeen (holy warriors). As far as I know, neither the U.N. nor the U.S. made any official response to Hezbollah's statement. I wanted both of them to get angry at the terrorists. I had hoped they would retaliate, demanding again and again that Rich be returned. I was angry, and I wanted to see them outraged. I wanted to walk into a meeting with the State Department or the U.N. or the Department of Defense and see just one of those bureaucrats slam his fist on his desk and say to me, "We will get your husband home! Rich will not be abandoned!" Instead, what I got was a hollow decree, a neatly penned official statement with no teeth. The resolution was quietly tucked away in an archives building, not living on the lips of the policy-makers. It had been recorded and shelved like the minutes of a meeting.

Why couldn't anyone be adamant about Rich's return? Didn't they understand that he put his life on the line with the complete confidence that he had his country and the U.N. behind him? I wished that I could make them understand how deeply Rich believed in his mission, that no matter how desperate his situation became, he would never stop believing that the U.S. and the U.N. supported him. I wished that I could make them see that wherever he was, even if he were hurt, hungry, and scared, he knew that they were fighting for him. His faith in them was unconditional, and their support for him was limited at best.

I tried to imagine what Rich would have done if it had been another officer who was captured. He would have taken it hard, suffering for the man and grieving with his family, just as he did when Captain McCarthy was killed by the roadside bomb. He would have fought for action like Resolution #618, but he never would have let it die. It wouldn't have been merely words on a page to him. It would be a commitment to his military brethren, a promise sealed with his word.

Sadly, there were so few people like Rich calling the shots. There were individuals in both the U.N. and the U.S. government who stood behind Rich, but in both cases, the whole was not the sum of its parts.

A few individuals couldn't force the U.N. officials or our own government into action. As agencies, neither the U.N. nor the U.S. made Rich and the other hostages a top priority. They were in the news only when people like Peggy Say or events like the adoption of the U.N. resolution caught the media's attention. Otherwise, they were subtly moved to the back burner, and the momentum fell apart.

As the impact of Resolution #618 dissipated, I began to view the U.N. as I did the State Department. Neither agency had a strategy, nor was either devising a plan. There was no action, only reaction. That is, the only policy both the U.N. and the U.S. followed was to give a response to the terrorist act by saying, "We don't negotiate with terrorists." If asked why, the answer was always, "We don't want to emphasize their importance." But it was no secret that, like it or not, they were important, and everyone — including the terrorists — knew it.

Terrorists are not reasonable people. Clearly, petitioning them to release their captives won't work. I wondered if they were ever going to seriously consider the U.S. or the U.N. as long as we continued to abide by our idle "policy." For my and Rich's sake I had to tell myself that they did take us seriously, but I couldn't imagine that they were threatened at all by our efforts so far. Did these radicals consider our written statements timid? Did they laugh at our carefully phrased resolutions and our attempts at diplomacy, knowing all the while that we were waiting for them to make the crucial moves? We were never going to get something for nothing from Hezbollah; we were fooling ourselves by saying that.

Even though I'd been disappointed by the U.N., I still trusted the Secretary General, Perez de Cuellar. Every time I met with him, he seemed ready to act and willing to stand behind Rich as a U.N. man. Over the preceding months, others had labeled Rich as an American officer on loan to the U.N., dismissing the fact that he was both an American officer and a U.N. officer. With that attitude, no one felt wholly responsible for Rich, and his fate could be conveniently passed from one hand to the next. De Cuellar didn't pass the buck. He understood that without him, I might not ever see my husband again, and he wanted to help.

The Secretary General respected my determination and my dedication to Rich. I'd like to think that's why he addressed the release of hostages whenever possible, lobbying to have Rich's name at the top of the list even after the State Department had swept Rich under the rug. Ultimately, though, I think de Cuellar sensed my anxiety. I always stayed composed around officials, and I never lost control. What little headway I did make would never have happened if I had been hysterical. They seldom looked into my eyes anyway. Sitting behind their desks or around conference tables, they looked above me, over me, or around the room, checking their watches in nervous anticipation that I might discover what I already knew: Nothing was being done to get Rich home. So it was easy to hide the fear, even the horror, that I felt most days.

De Cuellar, though, must have sensed what I was hiding. He looked into my eyes, and he listened. And if he had even a small taste of the panic, loss, and hurt that I kept inside, perhaps that's why he stood behind Rich. He understood why I had to fight for him.

I had to channel my energy and keep myself busy. As the days went by, Rich's capture became more and more consuming. His absence was a void that haunted me, growing more ominous by the day, threatening to swallow me whole. But at the same time, Rich was with me always. In my mind I saw an image of a smiling, healthy Marine in my mind. He was leaning against the rocks wearing his blue U.N. beret, like the picture that I gave to the press on the day of his capture. I filled my head with this picture. I had to. That man was my strength. He was the reason I was able to get out of bed in the morning and go alone through the motions of the day. The other images of Rich, the ones staring at me from the morning paper, couldn't really be him. He was gaunt and unshaven. When I studied his face for signs of my husband, I saw a tired, disoriented man. So I crowded my brain with a vision of the strong, suntanned officer. He was the one who would come home to me, and if I thought about stopping or giving up for one minute, pictures of Rich hungry and hurting crept into my head. They were unbearable.

August 7, 1988

*Today Iran and Iraq agreed to a cease-fire.
Secretary General Perez de Cuellar says he may be able to
announce the date of a cease-fire as early as tomorrow,
and it may take effect in two weeks. Two hundred and fifty
U.N. troops are to go in to observe the truce. I've got to
believe that the Secretary General's personal commitment
will get you out before then. There is word from Beirut
that the fate of the hostages may be linked to peace in the
Iran-Iraq war, that Iran has definite control over the
hostages, and that some of the hostages are being held in
the Iranian Embassy in Beirut.*

*Today I felt very sad for you. You must be so
frightened. You must've been hurt. And I'm scared and
hurt for you. Why would someone hurt you? You are the
kindest man on earth. I love you so much and I hope my
love for you will help to cure you when you get home. The
next two weeks are going to be hard for me — I hope they
are not hard for you. I hope they know you are going to be
released and so they are cleaning you up and fattening
you up and letting you go out in the sun. Don't be
frightened. Think of coming home.*

It had been nearly six months since Rich had been kidnapped, and
by then I should have learned not to get my hopes up. I should have known
not to rely on officials or agencies or departments to bring Rich home. It
only made each disappointment harder to bear, but the talk in early August
of an Iran-Iraq cease-fire gave me hope. I couldn't help feeling a little
high. The time seemed ideal for Rich's release.

The U.N. had called for a cease-fire between Iran and Iraq and
orchestrated peace talks between the two countries. De Cuellar negotiated
the terms of the cease-fire, and I thought for sure Rich's release would be
a significant part of it. In order to entice Iran into the agreement, the U.N.
offered to establish an Iran/Iraq Military Observer Group (UNIIMOG). It
would function like other U.N. observer groups by monitoring the fighting
zones between the two countries and giving Iran some protection against

the more powerful Iraqis. The U.S. supported the cease-fire and UNIIMOG. Congress even allocated funds to the U.N. for that purpose.

I thought this meant that Rich would be returned for sure. He was, after all, a member of the very force that the U.N was offering to establish in Iran. If they wanted UNIIMOG, then Iran would have to release the hostages. Both the U.S. and the U.N. had perfect leverage: no freed hostages, no U.N. protection.

The cease-fire was to become effective around August 20, 1988. I was told by U.N. officials that Rich would be home before that, maybe by the tenth. Perez de Cuellar was still working on Rich's behalf. Now that the U.S. had provided money to be used to help Iran, I was certain that the State Department and Department of Defense could and would use that as a way to demand Rich's return. Otherwise, how could they justify allowing U.S. money to be used to help a country that was holding an American soldier hostage?

That first week in August, I wrote:

> *Am I doing what Mrs. Stockdale warned against? Am I fooling myself into hearing what I want to hear? It's possible. Inwardly I'm encouraged, "gladdened;" outwardly I'm nervous and distracted. I don't want to wait until November — I want you back this weekend.*

> *Am I suffering from the "Stockdale syndrome" as I call it? Are you coming home; am I getting vibes, messages; or is my mind playing tricks on me and am I about to be really disappointed? I got a hopeful call from the White House and the U.N. yesterday. Then I saw a message from UNTSO about logistics after you're released. It's time, Richard, it's time for the Iranians to make their move. All that's left is for the Hezbollah to say, "We will release the spy Higgins at the request of the humane Islamic Republic of Iran." That's what I'm waiting for. I just don't see how the U.N. can accept any less — and send more U.N. troops to the Mideast, to Iran.*

In one of the most amazing indications of what overwhelming faith can do, I remember reading that Sybil Stockdale found herself putting pieces of reports and meetings together: "The mind is a marvelous machine, and once the imagination takes hold, it can really work up a head of steam. In my case, all sorts of things from then on became 'clues' that further confirmed my discovery."

I let myself believe that the whole nightmare would be over in just a few days. This was what I called "the Stockdale syndrome." Even when I was told it would be longer, maybe a month and a half, November at the latest, I knew Rich would be home soon, next to me, and I would be whole again. I could crawl out of the bubble I had been living in, where work, friends, family, and the Corps existed apart from me. They floated by, and I watched as if from a window, too far away to reach out and touch them. They moved so slowly, almost inert, as if time was quietly stopping while I hardly noticed. There was no meaning and no reason without Rich. I simply waited for the next event to happen.

I awoke each day to my clock radio giving reports about a kidnapped Marine, and the words rang in my ears, reverberating in my mind for hours. I ended my days with the pictures from the TV news. They showed photos of Rich pasted onto the screen, poised over the shoulder of a newscaster. The image was blinding, lingering on the screen until it became the only thing I saw. Rich became all I could really feel. Every emotion I had, every thought that touched me, concerned him. The people and events of my life merely hung in the background. It wasn't until I had Rich home that I could reach out of this cocoon and resume my life. Only then could the world be normal.

Would it ever be normal again? Each day in August ticked off the calender, and still no definite information about the hostages. I began leaving work early. I had no initiative there. Nothing interested me but news of the cease-fire and Rich's release. I had let all my hopes rest with the U.N. The U.S. government was almost completely out of the picture. They hadn't jumped on the opportunity to demand Rich's return like I thought they would have. They insisted that all hostages be on the table when there was talk of release.

I understood the principles of their position. They couldn't exhibit more willingness to work on behalf of one hostage than another, but Rich wasn't just a hostage. He was a POW, a soldier who had been kidnapped in a hostile nation. Most other hostages had stayed in or traveled to Lebanon despite the warnings and urgings by the U.S. government to leave. They were there as civilians and by choice. Rich was there on a military assignment. I didn't want him deemed more important than the others, but I did want him recognized not only as a hostage, but as a prisoner of war. The lives of the others were just as valuable as his, but nothing can change the fact that when Rich was kidnapped, he was serving both his country and the U.N. As far as I was concerned, he was being abandoned by both. My journal entry read:

> *I feel like I'm at war with the State Department. I believe I have uncovered a real philosophical disparity in our government — some see the military as cannon fodder, men who put themselves at risk and are expendable, willfully sacrificing themselves for a greater good (which is what?). We see ourselves as a little different — I think the man in uniform doesn't put himself at risk merely to sacrifice himself, but to subjugate his own self-importance to a higher ideal — but he can do that only because he believes in his country, that America does not leave its men on the battlefield. America is not fulfilling its loyalty oath to you. That is unacceptable to me.*

The State Department, however, stuck to their policy of "all or none" when it came to freeing hostages. Even though they had leverage during the cease-fire, they refused to act on it. If it wouldn't bring all of them home, then it wasn't important. I had lobbied for the Department of Defense to get behind the case since State was doing nothing, but Defense dragged their feet as well. What they failed to understand was that there were circumstances surrounding Rich's situation that made him different from the others. When an opportunity to use those circumstances to Rich's advantage arose, namely threatening to withdraw financial support of U.N. endeavors to aid Iran unless a U.S. Marine was released, our government should have capitalized on it.

Perhaps State was afraid of the negative media attention people like Peggy Say would bring to the government for "singling out" one hostage. Perhaps the Department of Defense was unwilling to see Rich as a POW since he was on a peacekeeping mission. Whatever their reasons, neither seized the chance to demand that Rich be released. So I played the waiting game.

By the 10th of August (the day I had hoped Rich would be home), U.N. troops were heading to Iran to prepare for the cease-fire. The U.N. sent me a message that they were "guardedly optimistic" about Rich's return. I was stunned. "Guardedly optimistic"? He should have been home that day, and now they were telling me they were hoping that they might get him home. My heart sank. I felt like the U.N. had been my last hope. Their chances to get Rich back were slipping through their fingers, and I was watching. I could see him falling farther and farther away from me, through a thick darkness until I could barely see him. It was pulling him down and away from me. When I realized that soon I wouldn't see him at all, I wanted to fall in after him. Near the end of August, it all caved in on me:

> *Rich, if I have to go on living like this — I can see myself committing suicide. Really. What an intense, amazing feeling of sadness and loneliness. I could feel tears welling up in my eyes all day, but they never fell. Even now my eyes are moist, but I'm beyond crying. I'm catatonic, I'm numb. I can't bear it too much longer without you. And I'm not just aching for me, although I'm terribly lonely. I am aching for you, dear. You are too kind, too wonderful to bear what you're bearing. Too proud, and rightfully so, to bear the degradation, the humiliation of having your freedom taken. Rich, I hurt for you.*

Chapter 12

Courage Is a Lonely Business

Month 6
August 20, 1988

> The cease-fire between Iran and Iraq was carried out despite the fact that neither the U.N. nor our government had any concrete information about the hostages. In fact, there had never been an ironclad agreement with the Iranians. I was led to believe that releasing Rich had been an initiative at the U.N. peace talks, but Secretary General de Cuellar had not received any guarantees from the Iranians that their friends, the Hezbollah, would free anyone. It appeared as though the U.N. had simply trusted that Rich and the others would be released.

It was hard to believe that they could have actually taken on faith that the Hezbollah, one of the most extreme terrorist factions in the world, would return Rich as a goodwill gesture. It seemed ridiculous to consider. Terrorists would never willingly cooperate with the U.S. or the U.N. We were their enemies. Furthermore, the U.N. had taken on faith that the

Iranians would do the right thing and act to have Hezbollah release their stranglehold.

I asked myself, why? Why had officials counted on Hezbollah to give Rich to us? Why did we wait for them to make a move instead of taking action? Why give the Iranians what they clearly needed and not exact a quid pro quo from them? It was clear to me, and I'm sure to Hezbollah and the Iranians, that the U.N. and the U.S. government were letting them call the shots. We were only responding, not being proactive, not retaliating.

And why didn't the U.N. or the U.S. anticipate Hezbollah's refusal to return Rich and Iran's intransigence on this issue? Shouldn't the Secretary General have been prepared for Iran to come up empty-handed on his specific request for "his hostage," the sole U.N. hostage, even if Rich's release wasn't among the "guarantees" that the Iranians gave the U.N.?

The questions that remained after the U.N. had all but assured me of Rich's return and failed, were nearly as hard to deal with as his continued absence. I had let myself be too optimistic, believing that since the U.N. claimed Rich as one of their own, they wouldn't stop until he were home. As it turned out, the U.N. was just another impotent bureaucracy, like the State Department and the Department of Defense. I had been so disillusioned, and the pain of the disappointment was more profound this time than ever before. August marked six months since Rich's capture.

I had played the moment back, on February 17th, a million times in my head, beginning with the shrill ring of the "bat phone." Every eye in the room watched Dan Howard's hand lift the receiver. The quiet was so intense I heard the clock on the wall ticking off the seconds. Dan looked straight ahead, not at any of us, and his mouth moved slowly, responding to the voice on the other end. He set the receiver back in the cradle, and the memory of his words assaults me. They fell out of his mouth slowly, but once loose, they rushed at me, pinning me to the seat. I've heard the words over and over, listening as they form a sentence that becomes more exacting each time; every syllable shining and sharp, cutting straight to my heart and twisting violently again and again so that I don't forget the pain. "We've got a problem. A Marine lieutenant colonel working with the U.N. was just taken hostage in Lebanon."

The memory of that morning is seared into my brain, and some days it runs on constant replay. I can recall nearly every detail, the clock on the wall, the coffee I was drinking, the expressions on each face in the room. I remember the sudden realization that this precise moment was the first time I had thought of Rich in two hours. He had needed me earlier, and I wasn't there. He must have called for me, but I wasn't listening.

The emptiness set in then, a deep, dark loneliness that was laid across my shoulders like a shroud. As heavy as it was, I never believed it would be forever. I have no memory of thinking that I would never see Rich again. If I ran each thought back through my head, playing them like a videotape, I know there wouldn't be even a second of doubt flashing across my mind. Rich would come home to me. Six months ago, I would never have dreamed I would still be without him.

Even more incomprehensible than that was the idea that nothing concrete was being done to bring him home. I was convinced that I was the only one that cared and that the U.N. and our government were deaf, dumb, blind, and heartless.

August 25, 1988

> *Tonight I go to bed with no hope of seeing you soon. How sad and lonely I am. I'm working so hard and I'm spinning my wheels. I spend most of my time fighting the State Department. I'm just trying to help — I'm smart, I'm willing to work, I never say this is how it should be, but I probe, I ask, I put one in touch with another. But as soon as I go down one road, another closes up. I hope you're doing better than I am.*

Although I was frustrated with the U.N., I was furious with the State Department. After the U.N. showed me that there was little they could or would do to find Rich, I had no choice but to turn back to State for help. I had learned over the past six months that any information I came across when dealing with the U.S. government would have to be painstakingly extracted. I was in a better position than other hostage families, though. My military background and connections at least made small chinks in the government's armor, and I was able to see and do more than the average civilian.

Unfortunately, the State Department often failed to consider me anything more than a civilian. Perhaps they forgot, or maybe didn't know, just how closely I had worked with military intelligence, the press, and high-level people throughout the Pentagon. I wasn't easily discouraged by their closed doors, nor was I fooled by political jargon and double-talk, and I dealt with a lot of both when I talked to anyone at State. I just couldn't trust them anymore. I saw through their sympathetic expressions and heard the hollow ringing of the "policy" that they recited in condescending, official tones. I couldn't take them seriously anymore.

To get any information at all, I had to first contact Mike Mahoney, the designated liaison between hostage families and the government. All questions and concerns of hostage families were funneled to him. His purpose was to interpret the news and report government findings to the families. In my opinion, Mahoney was there simply so that there would be someone to answer the phones when a frantic family member called. Mahoney was a gentle, kindly man, who spoke and listened more like a priest than a government bureaucrat. I'm sure that's why he was selected to do that job.

I always doubted the extent of his influence, however. I never felt like he had any real decision-making authority and certainly was in no position to create any sort of policy. There were definitely a lot of people who knew more than Mahoney and had access to the pertinent details I was after. So his lack of information was often the first roadblock I had to get over whenever I began another search for more answers. Luckily, I was persistent and had some good connections, or I never would have made it past Mahoney.

Most hostage families didn't, and we all had to deal with him a good bit. He seldom had significant information for me, but by August, he was one of a dwindling number of viable contacts that I had left at the State Department. He might have been the guy just there to answer the phones, but I couldn't alienate him. He was one of the only things I had going for Rich. I wrote in my journal that summer:

> *I voiced my displeasure and confusion to Mike Mahoney at State. First, I listened to his story, knowing what it would be — to knock down any rumors I saw. His purpose is to interpret the news; his net effect is to negate*

any positive news at all. His message is clear — we are doing nothing. I told him we should be more proactive, especially in the case of a military man on orders. He said that is a matter of debate within the Department. Damn, if the Department can't even agree, then where are we? We are waiting for someone to approach us; why not approach them? Then they will know they've got something we want. Damn, right. He said American public opinion would not be in favor of giving anything to the Iranians. I just don't know — American public opinion is a media monster and will do whatever the media wants it to do. The net effect is that everyone is afraid to do anything. And we sit here being shamed, because we're too big, high, and mighty to approach Iran like men and tell them we want an honest deal to bring our men home.

Mahoney's answers to my questions were useless, nebulous statements about "public opinion" and "policy," but talking to him sometimes helped me get my foot in the door, if nothing else. He simply didn't have the authority to affect the State Department or the Department of Defense. I knew that it was nothing personal. In fact, Mahoney was a very nice man, almost fatherly, in the way he dealt with hostage families. I'm sure that the State Department thought he might allay our fears by reassuring us that our government was on top of the situation. Perhaps they hoped that Mahoney's demeanor would help hostage families to trust the government. Then they wouldn't be like me, probing, searching, and always looking for ways to force our country to take responsibility.

Because Mahoney was kind, I never interpreted his attitude as indifference. I never believed that he withheld news or acted maliciously against Rich and the other hostages. He simply didn't have all the news we needed. There were others, however, who weren't as innocent as Mahoney. They worked from a negative agenda riddled with barbs that they aimed directly at Rich.

Of course, since Rich was a military man who had worked for the Secretary of Defense, he had his detractors. There would always be people within the Beltway who would twist his ties to the Pentagon into something that they weren't. Those were the same individuals who were willing and ready to run to the media with their stories.

Besides the people within our own government, there were those outside of the government who refused to acknowledge the fact that Rich had put his life on the line for them. Reports, like those from U.N. spokesman Timor Goksell that labeled Rich a reckless cowboy, still haunted me. I couldn't help but think that those statements, made soon after Rich was kidnapped, continued to hinder the effort to bring him home. People who didn't know Rich, those who believed everything they read in newspapers and magazines, were likely to believe a high-ranking official like Goksell. I knew what the public was thinking: Why should we support a man who went to a dangerous country and flouted the rules?

After six months, I thought I had developed a tough skin to statements like those made by Goksell. I wasn't immune to negative rumors and bad press, but I handled it and tried to accept that people in the government and the U.N. would print and say things that weren't true. It took months of disappointment and frustration, but finally I realized that they weren't all good guys. I would never fully trust the U.S. government or the U.N. with the same blind faith that I once had. They had not only betrayed Rich, but they had let me down as well. I gave them my husband, the most important thing in my life, and they didn't bring him home.

No matter how betrayed I felt by the U.S. or the U.N., I was sure that I would always have the unflinching support of the Corps. I was wrong again. A lieutenant colonel who had known Rich for many years was the lieutenant colonel assignment monitor at Marine Corps Headquarters. This man's job was to match up lieutenant colonels with jobs available and give them orders. When Rich applied for the U.N. position, he had wanted Rich to be sent from the Secretary of Defense's office to a more menial job on Okinawa, not to the prime job in the Middle East. The UNTSO position was not usually assigned to a Marine, so when Rich was asked for by name from the Army and the Department of Defense, it spoke very highly of him as a soldier. It meant that not just the Marines, but the Army and the rest of the military community had a great deal of respect for his work. It also meant, to this assignment monitor, that he was going to get railroaded and that he wasn't going to get his way.

This man was angry that Rich was given the UNTSO position. In my opinion, it was petty jealousy. He didn't like Rich and his success, which is why he pushed for Rich to get the less high-profile assignment at Okinawa. When he didn't get his way, he wanted to get back at Rich. He said that Rich had pulled strings to get the job, continuing to make this claim for months after Rich was captured. It was a power thing, and his way of tearing Rich down was to spread rumors about him when he wasn't here to defend himself. This man played the same childish power game as Goksell. Rich didn't do things their way, so they decided to pound a nail into his coffin.

I tried to get this fellow Marine officer fired or even court-martialed, but it never happened. I wrote a memo to the Assistant Commandant, but he was never punished for his actions. I was deeply hurt by what he had done. This wasn't another bureaucrat in a suit. He was a Marine like us. He was among our "band of brothers," a man we were supposed to be able to look to in the thick of the battle. Even if he didn't like Rich's success or agree with his career moves, he should have stood by him, and he should have supported me. Instead, he had breached the most sacred of military bonds: He left a fellow soldier on the battlefield — and shot him in the back while he was out there. I often wondered if men like him, who were so willing to turn on those they were sworn to support, had ever faced a life-and-death situation. Had he ever been scared and hurt and turned to the person beside him for help? Had he been alone like Rich, in a hostile country, aware that unless another Marine came for him, he could die without ever seeing his family again? If people like this man and Timor Goksell took just a second and tried to comprehend the terror and loneliness that Rich and I lived through on a daily basis, perhaps they would realize how cruel their actions were.

As I marked the sixth month of Rich's capture, I knew finally that I couldn't trust anyone but myself to fully protect Rich. Our own government had not circled their wagons, and it seemed that no one, not even a fellow Marine, was above cutting Rich down with lies and rumors that found their way to the press.

Aside from this one man, I wasn't aware of any other Marines who had turned their backs on Rich, although I now knew the unthinkable was entirely possible. The Corps, as a whole, was invariably behind me, and men like Commandant Al Gray were a source of unending strength, even if powerless to effect the change I sought. I still believed that no matter how cold and indifferent our government and the U.N. became, I would always have the support of the United States Marine Corps. Men like this small-spirited assignment monitor were there, but I would never let myself believe the Corps was infected with them. Marines were men and women willing to stand up for what and who they believed in. U.N. and government officials, I had found, were not so bold. They hid behind their titles and positions, moving like robots through their offices, sealed off from the pain of the real world.

Marines, on the other hand, wouldn't hide in the government's shadows. They stood out front, often leading the charge, as Rich had done in Vietnam and then with UNTSO. While our officials were safely tucked away in agency office buildings, Marines sat in muddy trenches or walked miles in the heat of a foreign sun. They tasted the dirt, sweat, and pain of life, and so did the families they left behind.

This common experience united Marines and their families and, indeed, soldiers throughout the world. Like Rich told the families of OGL after Captain McCarthy was killed, "We are all a part of a long line of honor, courage, and mettle. That line binds one soldier and his family to every other man, woman, and child that is a part of the military community. When tragedy strikes, those that are hurt and those of us who are left behind should be spirited by the strength of this military lineage."

September 7, 1988

Today a nice thing happened. I've been having trouble with the car. I think it's the bearings. I was going to go to Midas, because I know they have a reputation, but for ease and so I wouldn't have to rely on anyone else, I went by Lake Ridge Mobil. The guy must've recognized my name, asked if I'd heard anything about my husband, asked how my daughter was doing. He said not to worry, he's a retired Marine, I should bring my car to him and he'd take care of it. That's how community spirit should be, that's how Marines should be. He cared for me today.

Men like the assignment monitor tore at the fabric of the military family by persecuting their comrades. He might have worn a Marine uniform, but he was driven by his own misguided personal and professional jealousy.

As long as there were the likes of these mean-spirited ones, powerful men operating from their own agendas, I had to counter their actions with work of my own. I went to the Army. They were the executive agent for the Defense Department's support for the U.N. Bruce Mackey was a lieutenant colonel who had previously served in the Middle East, had guided Rich in his new job, and had the task of overseeing what was going on with UNTSO. Since he worked closely with the U.N. and the Department of Defense, I thought he could tell me why there had never been an official investigation by either the U.N., the Defense Department, or the Army. He was, after all, a colleague of Rich, and with his connections, I assumed he'd be willing to give me solid answers. Early on, he had been a real ally and go-getter.

However, by this time Mackey seemed changed. He was distant, even hostile, toward me, and I had no idea why. He seemed to have no interest in spending time with Rich's case. His response to my questions about the investigation seemed apathetic. It was hardly what I wanted to hear. He said that the U.N. had planned to investigate, but they put it off so as not to influence the initial ground and air search. Later, it was decided (and he never specified by whom) that a probe would open up Rich to criticism for riding alone and "being out of bounds." I got the feeling that Mackey was being instructed by someone to distance himself from me. I never knew who or why.

Immediately, I negated Mackey's answers. First of all, Rich was captured in February. It was now early fall. His excuse that the U.N. didn't want to hinder the initial ground and air patrol didn't account for the months since then in which the U.N. still neglected to make any effort at a formal search. In addition, it didn't account for the failure of the Department of Defense and the Army to start their own search. Mackey's explanation that Rich would be opened to criticism was also weak. It was clear to anyone with knowledge of UNTSO regulations that Rich was not violating any security codes when he was kidnapped. Mackey himself was one of those who insisted on that point early on, and now he was hedging. Why?

It seemed that Mackey, once one of Rich's staunchest allies, was all of a sudden interested only in justifying U.S. and U.N. indifference and ineptitude, and September of 1988 was the last time I went to him for help. I struck him from my list of contacts, which was growing shorter by the day. Every time I lost a connection, my hopes sank a little more. Bit by bit, the future was looking more and more bleak.

September 8, 1988

I am so depressed. I really am. This is not even normal depression. I don't feel like smiling. I don't feel like being sociable. I don't want to do anything. I just want to be left alone. I am literally playing a waiting game. There is almost nothing left to do. I have a few more tricks left up my sleeve, but I have finally come to believe that nothing will work. I don't know when you're ever coming home or what you will be like when you get here, and I am (and have been) powerless to affect it. Rich, I love you so much — you are my whole life. I've always believed that; now I know just what that means. Except that I want to be with you and be here when you get back and help you and grow old with you; I have no other reason for living and feel I can literally blow my brains out. I'm tired of being brave and strong and of wishing the same for you. You are tired, too, of being brave and strong, I know — it's time to just hold each other and shield out the world. I have never felt so helpless, so useless, so empty as I do right now. I will cry for you and for me tonight.

For nearly seven months I had imagined Rich's return. He would emerge from the plane smiling, a little thin and pale, but still strong. I could feel his still strong arms around my trembling body for the first time, and I could hear his voice. He was telling me that he was home, assuring me that everything would be OK, and then the weight of my sorrow would vanish. The heavy, looming clouds that had darkened my world would dissipate, and I would see blue sky and feel the sun on my face again. We would go home and lock the doors, shutting out the rest of the world, and for those moments nothing else would exist. Only Rich and me.

That picture was slowly being replaced with another. It was me, alone, with my back to the world. My face was drawn and sallow, my shoulders heavy with the burden of pain, but my eyes forever fixed on something ahead of me. I walked slowly, with tired legs, toward it, hoping again and again that my eyes led me toward Rich. Each step put me one foot closer to bringing him home, but the road was long and growing darker. I began to wonder if I would ever come to the end of it, if I would ever find Rich, or if I would spend the rest of my life looking and searching alone.

Major Robin Higgins, press conference,
The Pentagon, August 8, 1989

Chapter 13

Hope Dies; Love Doesn't

Month 7
September 12, 1988

Dear Friends,

We need your help.

Rich Higgins has been missing in Lebanon since February 17, 1988. Efforts for his release have been slow and painstaking. We now have a "window of opportunity" that had not been open before, but we fear it is closing. Letters, telegrams, and phone calls can emphasize to some important people the urgency of the situation.

We are asking you to write to the President, to your senators and congressmen, to the Secretary of State, to the Secretary General and Iranian Ambassador of the United Nations, and to anyone else you feel can be of help. The following points are pertinent:

★ *Lieutenant Colonel Higgins worked for the United Nations as an unarmed observer of the truce between Lebanon and Israel — a mission of peace. The attack on Lieutenant Colonel Higgins was an attack on the United Nations' presence in southern Lebanon.*

★ *His kidnappers respond to influence from Iran — even now, they receive money and other support from Iran.*

★ *Iran needs the United Nations.*

★ *The United Nations' member nations and the Secretary General are helping Iran in its effort to end the Iran-Iraq war and save millions of Iranian lives.*

★ *The Secretary General has asked Iran to use its influence to release Lieutenant Colonel Higgins.*

★ *The United Nations has asked for and is receiving U.S. support for the peacekeeping effort in Iran. Iran is aware of and has accepted this support.*

★ *There needs to be pressure applied and outrage expressed from the American people to the U.S. government, from the government to the United Nations, and from the United Nations to Iran, to have Lieutenant Colonel Higgins released now.*

We are sending this appeal to hundreds of people. We encourage you to pass this letter along to people you know who care and to anyone you feel can help

We — Rich's friends and family — appreciate your efforts and your prayers. We hope we will be successful and that Rich will be returned to us safely and soon.

With thanks and hope,

Friends of Lieutenant Colonel William R. Higgins

Some useful addresses:

> *The President*
> *The White House*
> *Washington, DC 20500*

> *Honorable George P. Shultz*
> *Secretary of State*
> *2201 C. St., NW*
> *Washington, DC 20500*

> *His Excellency Javier Perez de Cuellar*
> *Secretary General of the United Nations*
> *The United Nations*
> *New York, New York 10017*

> *Ambassador Mohammad Ja'afar Mahallati*
> *Permanent Mission of the Islamic Republic of Iran to the U.N.*
> *622 Third Avenue, 34th Floor*
> *New York, New York 10017*

Initially, I was nervous about making such a wide appeal, but by mid-September, I had mailed nearly 1,500 copies of my "Dear Friends" letter. After my latest encounters with the higher-ups proved Rich wasn't their top priority, I knew that I was the only one willing to dedicate myself to rallying the troops. Still, I didn't want to appear confrontational. Even though the U.S. government and the U.N. were doing nothing to get Rich home, I didn't want to appear as their adversary. I didn't want the U.N. or the U.S. government to think I was pointing fingers at them. In my mind, they were the bad guys, and it was me against them, but I couldn't let my true feelings show.

What if I lost my temper, alienated the government and the U.N., and caused them to write Rich off, too? I knew now that they were capable of such callousness. I had spent the last seven months wading through the mud and muck of their apathy. How would I live with myself knowing that words from my mouth might have contributed to Rich's pain? I had to be careful about what I said and what I wrote. I had already let Rich down once. I wasn't there for him back in February, when he needed me most. I couldn't let him down again. Every move I made, every word I uttered had to be well thought out, precise, and conciliatory toward the U.S. and the U.N.

Next to missing Rich, restraint was the hardest thing. The anger seething in my chest wanted to boil over, scalding everyone who had fueled it in the past seven months, but I held it in. The venom that rose to my mouth nearly flew off my tongue hundreds of times, but I swallowed it down, tasting its bile sliding back down my throat. I held back because it was important that they see me as someone who could be on their side if and when they would do the right thing.

The last thing I wanted was publicly to seem like I was at war with the State Department. I did feel like I was at war, but I couldn't let it be known. Besides, it seemed more beneficial to Rich's cause to work from the inside, within the system, rather than standing outside the Pentagon or the White House talking to the media. I needed the respect of the government and the U.N., not their animosity or suspicion. I had spent so much time proving that I wasn't the irrational hostage wife they expected, the one who hysterically attacked the government and pointed fingers at any and every high-ranking official. I certainly didn't want the "Dear Friends" letter to look as though I was lashing out at U.S. and U.N. leaders.

After all, I hadn't started a campaign against anyone, not like Peggy Say, who publicly criticized the government every chance she got. One of my main objectives was to appear as supportive as possible of the U.N. and the U.S. while in public. If I didn't have anything positive to say, I kept my mouth shut.

Peggy Say, on the other hand, seemed to me to honestly believe that her brother should come out first, even though I knew he had been warned not to be there in the first place. She went on every news program and talk show that would have her, seemingly trying to convince America that Terry Anderson was the only true victim of the hostage crisis. She told the media that not only had he been abducted by terrorists, but then abandoned by a cruel, indifferent U.S. government. It seemed to me that she thought that since Rich represented the government, which had done so little to get her brother back, he was not as important as Terry. Rich, because he had devoted his life to protecting freedom and promoting peace, was less important than her brother. It just didn't make sense.

My letter-writing strategy was not designed to be a thorn in anyone's side. I simply wanted people to know that if they became angry, they could pressure officials into action. I wanted them to know the facts, the most important of which was that Rich was still missing. After seven months, Rich was seldom on the news and only occasionally in the papers, but he was still being held against his will. He was still a member of the U.N. peacekeeping force, a Marine, and he was still a United States citizen. The longer he was a prisoner, the easier it was for people to forget that he had been captured.

I saw the letter-writing campaign as a way to make Rich a fixture in the public consciousness. Our government officials would know that he had family and friends who kept fighting for him, that we missed him and grieved for him every day, and that if our country and the U.N. did their jobs, we could get Rich home.

It made me feel good to think that people around the country would be thinking about Rich. When they woke up the morning after reading the letter, he would be on their minds. Later, while behind their desks, they would be preoccupied by the images in their heads of a soldier, hungry and hurting, praying for rescue. Then at night, when they turned the lights out, and their own families were safe and warm, only a room away, they would think of Rich again. And they knew how it would tear them apart if Rich were one of their own, lost somewhere in the Middle East.

Perhaps they would tell their friends about it, bring it up while standing around the water cooler at the office, their brows furrowed, voices low, talking about the government and the United Nations. "Why don't they do more?" they would ask each other, deciding then to write one of the addresses included in the letter and thinking maybe other people might do the same. Which one? "The President," they would say. "We need to get that man home."

The letter-writing approach was one Rich would have liked. He loved to see people work as a team, taking the power to make things happen into their own hands. Because I knew it was the right thing to do, I wasn't very worried that it took even more of my attention away from work. In fact, I was becoming completely single-minded. I wrote to congressmen and former U.N. military observers, U.N. officials and the Secretary General, the President and his cabinet. Each letter was a lifeline I was throwing out to Rich. After sending fifteen hundred letters, I had spun a web that worked its way across the United States and back. Some even stretched across the Atlantic, searching and probing for Rich.

Eventually, one would connect. A letter would be placed in the right mailbox, and the hand that reached in to get it would belong to the person that would get Rich home. I knew that out of all those letters, at least one had to be magic. One would answer my prayers and make my dreams real.

> *It's 7 A.M., I have the day off — so I slept in. I had a marvelous dream about you, so before I forget it all, I want to write it down. The main thrust was — they let you come home for a day. First you called. I was walking in a park and there was a phone on a tree and it rang and it was you, telling me you were coming home. You said something else — I don't remember what. I remember wanting to call Harry or Norm and tell them, but I think I couldn't get through so I rushed home. Then you came. It was all so rushed. We didn't get a chance to talk about a lot — but you looked great. Your beard was neatly trimmed and you even looked like you had a tan, etc. You felt good. That was the big thing I remember — it was like they sent you so that we would see you were all right. We were at some sort of block party and I remember you had to leave (I had to wake up). I remember heading away from the party so we could be alone. I think I asked you if you were tortured. I woke up. But I laid here in bed, happy that I was with you. I felt that you had sent me a sign, that you were OK, Rich, and I believe it. I must believe it — that's what gives me strength. Thank you for sending me this sign.*
>
> *I feel a little lonely though, because I did not wake up with you. You are not here, and I am still alone. But so are you. And we are thinking of each other. I love you very much and we will be together soon. I hope.*

The magic letter never came. People responded, showing their support and willingness to write to the addresses I had given them, but Rich remained a prisoner of the Hezbollah. Still, I was buoyed by the stir my letters caused. People were thinking about Rich again, and it couldn't have happened at a better time.

On September 29, 1988, the United Nations Peacekeeping Forces were awarded the Nobel Prize for Peace. According to newspapers, they won for "their contribution to reducing international tensions and in recognition of the central part in world affairs the United Nations has come to play."[21] Secretary General de Cuellar and his staff were praised for their roles in peace talks and international relations, and de Cuellar called the award "a tribute to the idealism of all who have served this organization and in particular to the valor and sacrifice of those who have contributed and continue to contribute to our peacekeeping operations."[22]

It was as if the Secretary General was talking directly about Rich, and I hoped that wherever he was, Rich heard that the peacekeeping troops had won. He was in his 226th day of captivity, but knowing Rich, if he were aware of the prize, he would come home saying that the pain and suffering was all worth it. His work in the Middle East had not been in vain, and the whole world would understand exactly what the men and women of the peacekeeping forces were about. Everyone would see how committed men and women like Rich were to making the world a better place.

> *I feel like you won the Nobel Prize! The prize went to the U.N. peacekeepers. My first call was a little after 9:00 from Commandant Martiny, Ambassador Walter's chief of staff. He congratulated me — and you. It got better from that moment. When NBC asked to speak with me, I knew the time was right. You always said, "When it's right you'll know it." I talked to both NBC and CNN. Everyone, including the U.N., thought it was a good idea. My idea now is that the Secretary General should announce that you will collect the prize and it'll stay in Oslo until you return. And tomorrow the Iranians speak with the*

---

[21] Karen DeYoung, "Award Signifies Restoration of Organization's Prestige Around World, " *The Washington Post*, September 30, 1988.
[22] Ibid.

*Secretary General at the U.N. How can these idiots in
Lebanon continue to hold you now? I know the award is
not only to you, but as AP says — you are the best known
U.N. peacekeeper. And I wonder if you were not taken, if
the peacekeepers would have gotten so much notoriety?
As I say — one man can make a difference. You have.*

*Chrissy is very excited about it — she says it's
"awesome." And she says she misses you.*

*Congratulations — you've won a Nobel Peace
Prize. Your beautiful blue eyes were on every evening
show tonight. A Nobel Peace Prize. How strange is life.*

I had learned that anything that was positively connected to Rich,
especially something as monumental as the Nobel Prize, could somehow
be used to get him home. The award wouldn't be given to the U.N. until
the December 10th ceremony in Oslo, but what better way for the U.N.
to really show their dedication to peace by refusing the Nobel until Rich
was released. It would send a resounding message to the international
community that the U.N. was accepting responsibility for Rich's freedom,
and on a broader scale, the freedom of everyone under their protection,
whether it be a soldier or a civilian. If the U.N. meant what they said
about Rich being among the best of the peacekeepers they had to offer
the world, then he should be in Oslo to accept the award. I had nine weeks
to convince U.N. leaders that unless Rich were there, they shouldn't
take it.

In the meantime, the hostage debate had been ignited in the national
media once again. On October 1st The Washington Post reported that
rumors of a new hostage deal were being repudiated by President
Reagan.[23] The Nations, an English-language Israeli weekly, quoted
sources in Geneva saying that the U.S. and Iran had reached a tentative
agreement to release nine hostages. There were supposedly eight
Americans scheduled for release, but Rich was not among them. The
Iranians claimed to be unaware of Rich's location. A rumor surfaced that
he had been spirited away on a fishing boat. Another story had Rich in a
specific three-story building and yet another had him hidden away in

---

[23] Bill McAllister, "New Hostage Deal Denied, President Calls Report in Israeli Weekly Untrue,"
The Washington Post, October 1, 1988.

military barracks. I couldn't understand why the Iranians, supporters of the Hezbollah and orchestrators of Rich's kidnapping, didn't know where he was.

The President's denial was part of the standard "we don't negotiate with terrorists" strategy I'd come to know so well. According to White House spokesman Marlin Fitzwater, the government wasn't denying that people were talking to Iran about hostages, but none of them were U.S. officials. The State Department chimed in, too, and also said the reports were completely false. As usual, everyone stressed the "No deal, period!" policy, and they were even more vague and stand-offish than usual. Election Day '88 was nearing, and no one wanted to do anything controversial that might cost their party votes.

I knew what the terrorists were thinking. They released one hostage, an Indian, in early October, and it was rumored other hostages would follow. There would be no Americans. I was sure of it. The Iranians (or whoever held the Americans at this point) would release everyone but the Americans before Election Day in order to embarrass us in the national and international community. They would start rumors and make false reports about the hostages' whereabouts, conditions, and release dates. It was the kind of games they played, always wanting to make the U.S. government look confused and powerless. Usually they did just that.

> *I just cannot shake this fear and worry over you. Is something happening to you? Are you OK? I just wish I knew. I just wish they would let me be with you. We were meant to be together.*

> *Do you realize we're not doing anything to get you back? I am — I think I'm doing all I can, at least I have. But no one is doing anything. The best I can say is that the U.N. asked the Iranians to help. They said no. End of that. The U.S. is doing nothing. I've about reached the end of what I can do. No one is listening to me; no one cares. I'm just an irritant. But, I'll tell you, after Election Day, I will make my rounds again. Why can't the U.N. put pressure on Iran? Why can't the U.S. put pressure on the U.N.?*

*Everyone assures me there are a lot of people
working on this. What are they doing? When they "work
on this," what exactly do they do? Are we any closer
today than we were February 17th to getting you back?
The answer, I'm afraid, is no — in fact we're further.*

*You may want me to be calm, to be professional,
to work within the system, but Rich, the system doesn't
work. The system doesn't care about you. I do. I care
about nothing but you. I just wish I knew if you were OK.*

*I love you very much. Tonight's daylight-saving
time. Now we are seven hours apart, I think. So far, Rich,
you're so far — yet close. I want you back. I want you
back. I love you lots and always will.*

Again, in October, came the rumors that Rich had been killed.
NBC's Fred Francis, who had reliable contacts in the past, heard that
Rich had been killed back in July. Fred, who had become a good friend
of mine, said that he was in touch with one Iranian official who would
not deny the report, but he wouldn't confirm it either. At the U.N.,
Ambassador Marrack Goulding, Undersecretary for Special Political
Affairs, informed me that the Iranians were again saying that they did
not know where Rich was and couldn't find him. Beirut and Israeli
newspapers all confirmed that he was, indeed, missing, but no one knew
whether that meant missing alive or missing dead.

I knew he was still alive, and I told myself over and over that the
reports were just rumors. To Hezbollah, Rich was an important prisoner.
He represented a valuable U.S. and U.N. commodity due to his U.N. status
and the fact that he was an official representative of the U.S. government
and the Marine Corps. He was national news, and Hezbollah believed
that playing with his fate would give them the most leverage with the
U.S. and the U.N. They were holding the crucial cards, and they knew it.
Perhaps, they thought, if Rich were important enough to both the U.S.
government and the U.N., someone would negotiate for him. Then the
terrorists could make a trade: arms, money, a terrorist being held in another
country in return for Rich. I don't think they were totally convinced that the
U.S. was adamant about the "no deal, period" policy. If Rich were
important, someone would strike a deal.

If I hadn't believed that the rumors were only terrorist mind games, I would have fallen apart. I wouldn't have even been able to pick up the phone and call the people who had the information to discredit the stories. I would have been paralyzed, frozen from the inside out, unable to even lift myself out of bed. And then it would be over, the whole ordeal through. No more wondering, searching, and asking, but no more hope and longing either. No more dreams that might come true, no more prayers to be answered. There would be no Rich, no husband, no family. Even with him missing, there was still something here. There was the struggling and scraping, the endless questions and probes to fill up my day and keep the connection alive, even if it were only a spark. But if I knew he were gone, if I really believed it, then my life slid into nothing, and I became surrounded by the loudest, most incomprehensible emptiness.

So anything negative, any report that said Rich was hurt or dying, had to be confirmed again and again. If I didn't have concrete facts to support a story, then it was a rumor, and my job was to prove it untrue.

When no one could corroborate Fred Francis' report, I put it out of my head, but the rumors must have scared the White House. On December 2nd, *The Washington Post* reported that the Reagan administration had spent the last week withdrawing American military officers from patrol duties with U.N. peacekeeping units in southern Lebanon.[24] Unidentified officials said that Lebanon had become too risky, especially for Americans traveling through the country. At last our government was publicly acknowledging the fact that Lebanon was extremely dangerous and not worth the lives of American soldiers. Even more importantly, they were finally taking a stand against the bad guys, but I couldn't help but think it might be too little, too late.

The Reagan administration's decision was timed perfectly with a move of my own. For several weeks I had been working on an editorial piece to send to a major newspaper. As with my "Dear Friends" letter, I didn't want to seem abrasive, but I did want the readers to know what was really going on — or not — to secure the release of the hostages, namely Rich. Two days after Americans were pulled from U.N. patrols in Lebanon, the *New York Times* ran my editorial. With the U.N.

---

[24] Associated Press, "U.S. Pulls Out of U.N. Patrol in Lebanon: Risks Considered Too High After Marine's Kidnapping," *The Washington Post*, December 2, 1988.

peacekeepers at the forefront of national news, maybe people would read my article and understand the risk involved and realize that the U.N. must protect the men and women who, themselves, are asked to protect hot spots like southern Lebanon.

Before I sent the article to the *New York Times*, I secured the support of all of my bubbas and the approval of the Commandant of the Marine Corps. I wanted to make sure I was doing the right thing, or rather, not doing the wrong thing. Never previously had I gone public with much of anything except my "Dear Friends" letter, especially not an editorial telling the U.N. how to do their job. My editorial piece let people know that Iran had no respect for the U.N. or the Secretary General. When we dealt with the Iranian officials, we were not dealing with honorable people. I urged the readers to examine the actions of the U.S. and the U.N. Was the public going to allow Congress to disburse funds to the U.N. in order to send yet another peacekeeping force into dangerous, terrorist-ridden territory like Iran, Iraq, or back into Lebanon? Were the American people willing to support an organization like the United Nations, that itself wasn't willing to make any effort to secure the release of an imprisoned U.N. man like Rich?

I reminded people that the U.N. had spent years trying to ease tensions in the Middle East, and that U.N. personnel from around the world had made sacrifices to the cause. To our government's credit, they had sent the best men and women to work for the U.N. Nonetheless, the fact that neither agency was doing all it could to bring Rich and the other hostages home could not be refuted. The U.S. and the U.N. were powerful enough to get these people back. Why didn't they?

With the help of my bubbas, I had crafted a piece. As a dutiful soldier I shared it with the Marine Corps and with the U.N. beforehand. Naturally they really preferred I not have it published; the U.N. specifically said it might make the negotiation for the cease-fire more difficult — and could interfere in getting Rich out. So I held it. When it all began to fall apart, I once again felt betrayed — that the whole reason for their telling me a date certain, then for their "guarded optimism" was to stop me from going public. Once I realized this, I sent the editorial piece in and the *New York Times* published it.

At the time the editorial ran, the popular excuse for inaction was related to the turmoil in the Middle East. By December, fighting between Amal and Hezbollah had reached a fever pitch in Lebanon. Once the cease-fire with Iraq was carried out, a new dispute arose within Iran that concerned future associations with Western countries. Moderate leaders, with connections to Amal, supported the move toward improved relations between Iran and countries like the U.S. Because of the active role the U.S. and the U.N. took in engendering the cease-fire, moderate leaders seemed ready to work with the West on issues like releasing hostages.

However, radical Iranians with ties to terrorist groups like Hezbollah were staunchly opposed to any positive actions towards Western countries, particularly the U.S. The power struggle between the leaders of the two factions resulted in a serious increase in domestic battles. As long as the political climate of Iran was so highly charged, the U.S. and the U.N. shied away.

The Middle Eastern tensions also hurt my plans for the Nobel Prize award ceremony in Oslo. Over the previous weeks, I had talked to Secretary of Defense Carlucci, National Security Advisor Colin Powell, and several state department officials about accepting the prize only if Rich were also in Oslo to receive it. They all liked the sound of the idea, but no one was willing to carry it to Secretary General de Cuellar. The consensus was that in order to get de Cuellar to agree, they would have to beat him over the head with the idea, and none wanted to put that kind of pressure on him. There was too much anxiety over the fighting in Iran to make so bold a move.

So, the award was accepted on December 10th without Rich. The Secretary General did make an appeal for Rich's release, and although it restored a little of my faith in him, the appeal was heard by no one, and no one cared.

Perhaps de Cuellar could channel the international momentum and enthusiasm from the award ceremony into support for action in the Middle East. Something had to be done, especially to calm the situation in Iran. Either the U.S. or the U.N. had to put a foot down and take the lead. If not, the fighting would spin out of control, and we would never have another chance to get a handle on it again. Already, every newspaper I read printed a story about the fighting, the utter chaos that was raging in Iran. Where was Rich? I saw him in the middle of it all, being tossed about like a rag doll in a storm.

Things were more frantic now, and the Hezbollah appeared more erratic than usual, reporting one day that hostages would be returned, and then trying to frighten us the next day by saying they wouldn't be released. No one seemed to know exactly what would happen next.

We got our answer on December 12th when a picture of Rich arrived in Washington. It was a photocopy of a photograph of Rich, similar to the one the terrorists released back in April. He was facing the camera, but his eyes were cast downward, away from the camera, and his shoulders hunched. His beard was only stubble, and he wore a dark field jacket. I told myself that his face looked fuller, that he was healthier than in the picture from nine months ago. Maybe they were feeding him well, letting him exercise and get healthy. It was a sign they would send him back to me soon.

Then I learned about the message that accompanied the photo. The Hezbollah, again calling itself the Organization of the Oppressed, was threatening to execute Rich for being an Israeli spy. In their statement, the terrorists said they would kill Rich in retribution for the latest Israeli raid on a Palestinian guerrilla base south of Beirut during which nine guerrillas were killed. He was their most important hostage, the one with the closest ties to the leaders of the U.S. and the U.N. In their minds, executing him rather than another hostage would make their vengeance even sweeter.

The Organization of the Oppressed said that "it had been proven by clear-cut evidence that [Higgins] and his American team of observers are guilty of providing the Zionist enemy with accurate and detailed military and security information about our resistance fighters, their positions, movements, supply routes and the quantity and quality of their weaponry." According to his captors, Rich's death would be "revenge for the blood of martyrs."[25]

---

[25] Farouk Nassar, "Kidnappers Vow to 'Execute' U.S. Marine Col. Higgins: Threat Linked to Lethal Israeli Raid Friday," *The Washington Post*, December 13, 1988.

Chapter 14

New Year, New Strategy

Month 10
December 21, 1988

This was the day I was hugged by the Commandant of the Marine Corps, the Chairman of the Joint Chiefs of Staff, Mr. Weinberger, Mr. Carlucci, Ambassador Walters, and Vice President George Bush!

It all started at 9:00 A.M. when I got a call from the Vice President's office asking if I could come over there at 1:00 P.M. to see Mr. Bush. The woman on the other line said that Ambassador Walters was there and he would pick me up. After that, my mind was Jell-O. I knew that Ambassador Walters had met with the Vice President that morning and was then going to see the Commandant.

I remembered that Sybil Stockdale said in her book that her morale, if not her life, began to turn around when she found a lone public official who went out of his way to be kind. In her case, it was then-Governor Ronald Reagan. Mine was about to be Vice President George Bush.

In the car on the way to the White House with Ambassador Walters, I tried to tell him how intransigent the U.N.'s Marrack Goulding was being with me, but he didn't seem to bother with Goulding. He told me the Secretary General himself was doing things. He said the Secretary General was trying to get someone in to see Rich by Christmas.

In the Vice President's office that afternoon, I was surprisingly comfortable. The Vice President strode in — he seemed to me energetic, youthful, attractive, and real. He said he wanted to meet me just to wish me happy birthday and a merry Christmas. He asked about the family. He told me that General Walters said he had met all the families and I am the bravest. Mr. Bush asked if I was being kept informed, and I praised Ambassador Walters and the Commandant. Mr. Bush said if on January 20th, when he became President, he could do anything to help, he would. I told him I believed him. It was magnificent.

And then, that very night, there was news of a terrible plane crash over Lockerbie, Scotland. I felt just sick for the Americans on board. I remember thinking, Rich is coming home, but these men and women are not.

Month 10
December 23, 1988

Oh, how I wish we were together tonight. We'd laugh and remember eleven years. I remember alone today — did you? This last year hasn't been a good one, but in many ways we have been closer this year than ever before. I know my mind — my every waking moment and many of my sleeping moments — have been filled with you. And of us — what it was like and what it will be like.

Chrissy invited friends over tonight for a birthday party — it was special — and bless her heart, she was afraid to mention anniversary. But I guess I don't get choked up, because I feel so close to you. I just hope that by my strength, and whatever courage I show, I am helping you. You must know that we are survivors. I hope we don't have too much longer.

I wonder where we will be on our next anniversary. Wherever it will be — we will be together.

Did Rich know what day it was? Was he keeping count somehow, marking off the hours, days, and weeks on a wall somewhere? Would he realize it was my birthday? Would he know that it was our anniversary, and I was spending it alone?

Last year we had spent our tenth anniversary together, in a hotel in East Jerusalem, excited about Rich's move to OGL and speculating what the future would hold for us. A successful mission with the U.N., maybe a regiment when he returned home and became a full colonel. Chrissy would go to college, and I would stay on at the Pentagon, waiting for Rich to return from the Middle East in June.

Now I was celebrating our eleventh anniversary (and my 38th birthday) without him, enraged at the nameless, faceless people who were keeping Rich from me. Eleven years was not enough time together. We deserved more, not another missed holiday or birthday. Our love warranted more than another milestone like our anniversary, more than yet another day that made the emptiness in my heart scream louder.

And it screamed with an anger and hate that I didn't know possible. The day that had once been the happiest of my life was now filled with a bitterness and loathing for everyone who had kept Rich and me apart. Beneath my anger lurked the ever-present terror that reminded me just how dangerous the people we were up against could be. They didn't care what we deserved or wanted or dreamed of. They didn't care that it was our anniversary or my birthday. They especially didn't care that in two days it would be Christmas. While everyone else went to parties, opened gifts, and spent time with their families, all I could do was pray that my husband was still alive.

I had hoped for good news on our anniversary. I wanted to hear that Rich was coming home. The terrorists had given in, and they were sending him to us for Christmas. Was it too much to ask for? Maybe. The miracle I was hoping for was too much like a movie script. Rich returning home for the holidays, just in time to start the new year with his family. And 1989 would be a clean, fresh start. We would leave the past behind, looking only toward the future and the rest of our lives.

Until Rich returned, the rest of this life would be on hold. I spent too much time spinning my wheels to consider moving forward, and the rumors of Rich's impending execution set me back even further. It had been eleven days since Hezbollah threatened to kill him, but no news since then.

As far as we knew, Rich was still alive. Hezbollah had bluffed before, trying to scare the U.S. and Israel. Terrorists were like schoolyard bullies, their tactics crude and childish. In other words, if the U.S. or our friends (i.e., Israel) hurt them, they would hurt us, and they would play dirty. I felt certain that if they did kill Rich, they would be quick to let the U.S. know. Hezbollah wanted to burn our government badly with their "revenge" and then taunt us with pictures and messages that recounted their perverse savagery. There would be nothing honorable or even human about the way they killed a hostage, and they wanted everyone to know it.

To Hezbollah, Rich wasn't just a prisoner. He was a spy, the most despicable of adversaries. They didn't care that he had a wife, a daughter, and a family who loved him. They didn't care what losing Rich would do to us. When they looked at Rich all they saw was an enemy. The most astounding thing about their claims that Rich was a spy was that they truly believed it, and as a result, Rich would pay for his "crimes." He would be the victim of Hezbollah's twisted, capricious evil unless we got him home. His life would end whenever they wanted it to.

I tried to understand how they thought, how the terrorists who took Rich decided he was a spy. I wanted to pry inside one of their heads for just a moment, just long enough to trudge through the depravity and the madness to the place in their minds that said Rich was the enemy. What could have made Hezbollah believe that an unarmed peacekeeper was really an assailant? I thought that if I understood what they believed that I would know how to get Rich home. I would know how to say and do the things that they wanted to hear.

But I couldn't do it. I couldn't understand them. The way terrorists thought was so foreign to me, so reprehensible, that it wouldn't possibly register in my brain.

The new year brought more fighting to southern Lebanon and south Beirut. Tensions were pulled tighter every day, which meant Rich was in constant danger. All it would take was one incident to set Hezbollah off, and who knew what it would be?

On January 4, 1989, the U.S. gave them good reason to retaliate by shooting down two Libyan planes. Libya was an ardent supporter of Iranian-backed terrorist groups, so I was sure Hezbollah would counter the U.S. strike with an act of their own. Since Rich was already on the top of their list, and he was the only American military officer being held hostage, I prepared for the worst. If they wanted to make the U.S. pay, they would take Rich.

Once again, we were all waiting, watching to see if the terrorists made a move. I hated playing their waiting games. I tried to tell myself that each day that passed wasn't another day we had been apart, but it was one day closer to our reunion. That way as days stretched into weeks, Rich moved nearer to me. It made days like January 8th easier to bear.

> *Right now — about 3 A.M. there — last year, we were getting up to go to the airport. I didn't want to go, I didn't want to leave you. That was the last time I saw you, honey. When will I see you again? Will it be in two weeks on Inauguration Day? It just does not seem like that will happen. Will it be in 1989? Will it be ever? I remember our last hug, our last kiss — it was bittersweet and full of love. But, I love you more now than I did then. I never would have believed that possible. But I do. You are not perfect; neither am I. I have not put you on a pedestal. But you are the man I love, that I admire, the man from whom I have learned more about life and love than anyone or anything else. I want to share with you the person I've become. More aware of my vulnerabilities, but more able to understand them and bear with them.*
>
> *You are too good for this to happen to you. I continue to believe that something good must come of this. I know one good thing for me is how much more I've come to love you. If our love can be stronger and better as we grow older together, that will be a good thing.*
>
> *Let's hope for that.*

Hope was nearly the only weapon I had left for 1989. My arsenal of contacts and strategies was depleted, and the conflicts in the Middle East put getting Rich home out of my control. All we could do was hope that the fighting stopped before it was too late to save the hostages.

For weeks Syria and Iran, supporters of Amal and Hezbollah, respectively, had been making attempts at a truce. Unfortunately, all talks usually ended in more disagreement and then more fighting. Toward the end of January, however, cooperation looked like a possibility, and on January 30th, high-ranking officials from both factions signed a truce. The agreement was intended to end the violence and to work toward the release of foreign hostages. In fact, paragraph eight of the agreement stated that all sides agreed not to touch either the U.N. forces in Lebanon or the members of the international organizations and missions.

It was good news for Rich. Since the fighting had intensified months earlier, he had been Hezbollah's pawn. They had threatened his life in order to prove their mettle to Amal, Syria, Israel, and allies of the U.S. Now that they didn't need to flex their muscles, they would release him. They had to. They had agreed to a truce that forbade them from taking and holding U.N. personnel. I expected officials like Amal leader Nabih Berri and Syrian Foreign Minister Farouk Charaa to say that all the hostages would be coming home as soon as possible. I wanted a date and a time. Instead, Berri said, "I can say I am sure this agreement will help the release of the hostages (as) quickly as possible, but I cannot say or give a date for that."[26]

Statements like that were too equivocal, and I didn't trust them. By now, I could spot disappointment before it hit me head on, and I knew not to rest my hopes on the new armistice. I did believe that since the truce stopped the fighting, it took Rich out of immediate danger. Hezbollah hadn't issued any new statements about the execution, so maybe Rich was safer than he had been a few months ago.

Still, the waiting was killing me. Even though the tensions between Amal and Hezbollah had cooled a little, neither the U.S. nor the U.N. was making a move. Furthermore, they had no plans to do anything. While

---

[26] Nora Boustany, "Syria, Iran Impose Truce in Lebanon; Halt in Shi'ite War Seen Aiding Hostages," *The Washington Post*, January 31, 1989.

they looked over Rich like he wasn't there, all I could do was the same thing I had been doing all along: sit by and watch them do nothing.

I had taken great pains over the last eleven months to work within the system. I endured frustration after disappointment after betrayal, and I never even considered going anywhere but to the "officials" for help. It is what Rich would have wanted, and, as a Marine who had a great deal of respect for the system of our government, I thought it was the best plan of attack as well. But with Rich missing nearly a year, I began to consider other channels.

Going to the mass media had never appealed to me because I'd seen the way Peggy Say and others had used it to single out one hostage. Also, the media were not above manipulating a story, especially in television, and I worked too hard collecting the facts to have them distorted by some evening anchorman. On the other hand, where else was I to go? It seemed like every possible channel had been exhausted. Every long, winding avenue had ended in a torturous dead end. It was time for a new plan of attack.

On February 17th, one year after Rich was captured, I was in New York preparing to do the morning news shows. I spent several days in New York and appeared on "Good Morning America" and "The Today Show." At ABC, I interviewed with Hattie Kaufman, then with Jane Pauley at NBC. They both asked how I dealt with it all: the time that had gone by, the rumors he would be executed, the frustration over the failure to get him home.

I could have ripped into the government and the U.N., told both women that I was the only person who was doing anything to get Rich home. I could have said that, even worse, no one cared about Rich. They had left him there a full year, and they would leave him there longer.

I didn't say any of those things. As always, I held back. I told them that I was optimistic about the truce signed in January, even though I really knew it would amount to nothing. It was just a matter of time before the fighting resumed, but I didn't say anything like that during my interviews. I couldn't bring myself to do it. I was still apprehensive that saying something negative would hurt Rich, so I was as supportive of the U.S. and the U.N. as I could be. I even told Jane Pauley that the U.N. kept me well informed.

Then she asked me why I had finally decided to come on television. She said that she had met other hostage families who, for one reason or another, had gone immediately to the media. She wanted to know why a woman like me, a private person with the ability to work within the system, would suddenly turn to television.

I wanted to tell her that I had no choice. Every other door had been slammed in my face. The media was the only door I thought was open.

Instead, I gave her the most diplomatic answer I could come up with. I said, "I only have one purpose and that is to bring my husband home. And I never felt that by my going on television or speaking out, it would advance the cause of bringing him home or his welfare. And today is an anniversary, and so I thought it very important — anniversaries are important. They're a time for new beginnings and rebirths."[27]

Did I really believe that? Rebirths and new beginnings meant things were looking up. They meant that the future was bright and wide-open. Was there a future for Rich and me? There were positive signals like Rich's promotion to colonel on March 1st. I took it as a sign that he was coming home. He had to return and finish his career, accomplish his goal of commanding his own regiment. The work in the Middle East hadn't been in vain because it had made him a better soldier, and other Marines were recognizing it. The promotion told me that the Corps believed in Rich, that he would come back to serve them again in the States. If other officers were that hopeful, then I could be, too.

Positive steps like that kept me going. For so many months I had considered myself to be going at it alone, but the faith and support of the Corps was always with me. They gave me the strength that I needed to keep my spirits up. Rich would come home soon.

I was also inspired by Sybil Stockdale. A couple of weeks after the news of the promotion, we met at a luncheon at the Quantico, Virginia, Officers' Club. I was always amazed at her stories of survival, both that of her husband and her own, during and after the years he spent as a POW. Sybil employed the same plan of attack that I had used at the beginning: work within the system. She fought doggedly for her husband's return, but she wasn't openly critical of government officials.

---

[27] NBC "Today Show," interview with Jane Pauley and Robin Higgins, February 17, 1989.

She also tried to learn from what was happening to her, knowing that some greater good had to come out of their ordeal. I told her that I felt the same way. Eventually, Rich and I would look back on all this and remember. The bad part will be over one day, just like Sybil Stockdale's nightmare ended when her husband came home. In a way, I felt like I was looking at myself 15 years down the pike. Perhaps I would be sitting beside a woman like me, a desperate wife, telling her not to lose her faith. She would look at me the way Sybil and I were looking at each other, with an understanding of the fear, the incessant loneliness, that plagued us.

My meeting with Mrs. Stockdale was one of the only occasions during Rich's capture that I made that strong of a connection with another person. Usually I reserved that intensity of feeling for communicating, writing, to Rich. Every night in my journal I spoke to him, letting out all that I held in during the day. Mrs. Stockdale gave me the same kind of hope that writing to Rich did. It was a strong, resilient hope, one that foretold joyous reunions, steadfast love, and growing old together. It stretched over time and place, pulling me closer and closer to Rich.

So with the help of the Corps and Sybil Stockdale, I decided that new beginnings were possible. My faith in the future was renewed, but my confidence in the government and the U.N. was not. I knew that I couldn't turn to them again for the answers that I needed. Relying on either agency would be setting myself up for more frustrations, and after more than a year we couldn't afford anymore lengthy setbacks.

I turned my attentions toward private initiatives. If going the official route wasn't working, then I needed to explore other options. For the past thirteen months, I told myself that there were two methods by which I could get Rich home. I could go to the mass media, or I could go through government and U.N. channels. It was one extreme or the other, and I didn't consider that there was anything in between until I met Ambassador David Miller, Special Assistant to the President and Senior Director of International Programs. Out of the blue, he called me to his office in the Old Executive Office Building, right behind the White House. Why did he call? Was it just his idea, or was he encouraged by George Bush or maybe Colin Powell? I never did ask, because I was just grateful he did.

He suggested that I consider getting a private attorney who would help with contacting people and putting together initiatives. He would be someone who I knew for certain was always pulling for Rich and me. Miller told me that he and his wife decided that if they ever experienced what Rich and I were going through that she should not stay inside the government. He shared my opinion that the government cannot and will not act. I wondered, then, why I stayed so long, but the truth was I trusted the U.S. and the U.N. Where else would I have gone except to the media? Miller even recommended a friend of his, and I promptly went to see him, a new excitement and a nervous fear of new territory clouding my steps.

Now, I was taking matters into my own hands, rather than politely waiting for people to call me back or fit me into their schedule. Greg Craig offered to do the work pro bono and jumped right into the thick of things. Greg seemed too young to be as smart and as powerful as he turned out to be. He was too energetic, too friendly, too personable to be a Washington lawyer. But he believed in me, and he believed in the cause. And he quickly joined my bubba group. They liked him as well.

By the end of March, Greg and I had met with Secretary of State Cyrus Vance, Ambassador Thomas Pickering (Ambassador Walters' successor as U.S. Ambassador to the U.N.), Senate Minority Leader Bob Dole's security affairs assistant, and other senior and influential officials to whom I never had access before.

Greg's initial agenda consisted primarily of asking Secretary of State Vance for his assistance in urging the Secretary General to redouble U.N. efforts related to Rich's release. Greg suggested that a special coalition be assembled within the U.N. with the special duty of following Rich's case. I liked his attitude. He said Rich was sent there by the U.N. and the U.N. should bring him home with help, of course, from the U.S.

Greg also proposed trying to find contacts in the Palestine Liberation Organization, especially since they had been instrumental in the past in getting hostages released. His most interesting proposal, however, was that we go overseas and try to establish an effective network of contacts in Europe. There, we would be away from the U.S. government, not working in its shadow, but completely apart from it.

The thought of going entirely outside of the government did make me nervous, but I was willing to consider it. There were still reports coming from Beirut about Rich, and I hated to turn my back on the officials who were receiving them. Sometimes the reports claimed hostages, including Rich, were to be released. Others stuck to the story of Rich's impending execution.

I listened to the conflicting reports over and over, and when I asked what was being done about them, no one knew. No one within the system could tell me what was true and what wasn't. They had no idea what was happening to Rich and the other hostages or what would happen to them. It was impossible to get a straight-forward, informed answer.

The rumors continued through the winter and into the spring, and after weeks of listening to the government posturing and speculating on the future of the hostages, I decided to go with Greg's plan.

In May, we traveled to London, where Greg had assembled a group of viable contacts, people that he believed had or could get pertinent information that might lead to some real action. Some of the men we met were directly connected to the Shi'ite movement. Jamil Mohammed was a seemingly powerful Lebanese businessman with a lot of strong connections, especially to Nabih Berri, the Amal leader who was then Lebanon's Minister of Justice. Another Lebanese we met was Kamil Khoury. He was a friend of Bishop Robert C. Witcher, the Bishop of Long Island and retired Navy chaplain. The bishop and I had been in contact before to discuss his Iranian ties. For months we had been writing and talking about people he knew who might help me get Rich home. He suggested Khoury might help. I also met with Patrick Seal, Syrian President Assad's biographer; a highly placed representative of the Archbishop of Canterbury; and Charles Glass, former hostage and ABC reporter.

The men knew a good deal about Rich, and each one seemed to respect what he had done in the Middle East. The contact with Jamil Mohammed seemed especially fruitful. We spoke with him privately, and then we shared a meal with his wife and sons. I needed to meet men like Mohammed, kind Shi'ites who wanted to see Rich back with his family. Mohammed was going to meet with Nabih Berri and, as evidence of his contact, would secure a picture, maybe even a letter from Rich. Even after Greg and I returned to the U.S., I continued to get news from our new contacts, assuring me that they were talking to people, sending letters, and gathering information for Greg and for me.

It was good to know that someone somewhere was working for Rich because I knew that besides Greg, Ambassador Miller, and me there weren't many others fighting for Rich. I hadn't been in direct contact with the government in so long, and the last news I heard from the U.N. had come months ago, back in February. It seemed that even the media had forgotten about the hostages, but if I had anything to do with it, America wouldn't forget.

I took opportunities like Memorial Day 1989 to remind people that Rich and others were still prisoners, still in danger of being hurt and even killed by terrorists. I gave a speech at Quantico National Cemetery urging my audience to remember not only the dead but the living. There were over eight hundred people there to listen to me tell them that America cannot forget the hostages being held in the Middle East. While we mourned that Memorial Day for the fallen, my message was we must pray for the captive.

A few days after my Memorial Day speech, I received my first call from Ross Perot. I knew that he had been outspoken about the hostage situation in the past. He advocated plans like privately funded rescue missions and negotiating with terrorists. Because I had taken the inside track and stayed within the system for so long, Perot and I had never spoken before. Until now, his methods had never been an option for me.

Perot agreed that the government and the U.N. could not and would not do anything. He told me that the burden of bringing Rich home was on my shoulders, and if I needed his help, I would get it. If they offered to release Rich in exchange for money, I should go to him, but he wasn't just throwing his money around. There was a strict "pay only on delivery policy" involved in Perot's strategy. His plan had four steps: 1) make contact with the captors, 2) negotiate, 3) work out an exchange, 4) "hope to get lucky." I knew that if and when Greg and our new connections made contact with Rich's captors, Perot would help us.

Breaking out of the system was beginning to look like it would pay off. I was talking to Ross Perot and keeping in touch with powerful Lebanese intermediaries. Greg was working on new contacts in Damascus and Syria, and my bubbas were always working on some sort of lead. Marine Commandant Al Gray and Ambassador Miller at the White

House continued to try and rally support for Rich in Washington. And I had even gotten the attention of President Bush. I had a real network going. It was so different from before, when I had only lip service and empty promises that "something will happen." Now, I felt like we were getting somewhere. There hadn't been any significant news about the hostages in weeks, but I wasn't waiting for news anymore. I was taking action, making things happen, and felt myself stepping closer to Rich every day.

Then on July 28, 1989, we hit a wall. The Israelis captured Sheik Abdul Karim Obeid, an important Hezbollah cleric in south Lebanon. The news media immediately tied him to Rich's kidnapping, but among my small circle of contacts, we had no independent confirmation of whether or not he was actually involved. Still, Hezbollah threatened to retaliate. If Israel didn't release Obeid, Rich would be hanged. I heard this before, but this time it was different.

> *I was told the Organization of the Oppressed on Earth has threatened to hang you if Obeid is not returned by 8:00 tomorrow morning. Israel, of course, will not do that. This is a tough one, Rich. Even Chrissy admitted she's upset by this one. It's fully what we expected—for every action, there's an equal and more deadly reaction. I expected a picture, though. But there's no way to brace yourself to hear something like that. And why no picture — are you already dead? Or are they trying to make us believe that? Or is it not the real group? My belief is it's the real group. I don't know why there's no picture. I think just to confuse us. So will they kill you? No. But I'll tell you, the U.N. and the Iranians better be talking right now. And the U.S. better be doing something. There's nothing more I can do to influence the action and I really don't need to know it all, but it better be happening.*

> *Richard, I love you. Be strong tonight — if they are serious, you are very scared tonight and you've got to know that I love you — always have and always will. I love you and thank you for making me strong. I hope I can help you be strong, too.*

The next morning Israel didn't release Sheik Obeid, and we braced ourselves, waiting for a Hezbollah reaction. They sent it on a videotape and said it was Rich. When I turned the television to CNN, I saw my husband's face first, then his limp body, turning at the end of a noose.

Chapter 15

Etched Into My Mind

Month 17
July 31, 1989

**Today has been ghastly. How do I characterize it? I am
in a daze and I don't fully understand the bizarreness of
what is happening. They say they killed you and the
man who appears to be hanging is you. All the emotions
of the first days have returned. I can't give up, but,
honey, I don't think we'll ever kiss again. Of course,
my feeling of loss is immense, my feeling of sadness for
Chrissy is great — but the loss for the world of a
wonderful person is most tragic. Good night —
I'll keep writing. I will not give up. I love you.**

For 17 months, my most painful memory, the one that plagued
my days and nights, had been the incessant remembering of February 17,
1988. The constant playback of Dan Howard's words, then the instant
knowledge deep inside that the course of my life had been altered
forever. It had veered onto a treacherous, unmarked path, and I was left
alone, searching and hoping for direction. But I knew there had to be a

clearing up ahead. I could even see it in the distance. I just needed to make it there. If I could just go a little farther, the road would be smooth again, bright and easy, and the change in my life only minor, the damage correctable.

That was before the atrocity of February 17th was replaced by another, when the gruesome, depraved image of Rich hanging by a rope became the picture that haunted my mind. It was now my most painful memory, pushing aside February 17th and the day I spent our anniversary alone and the time I heard the first reports months ago that Rich would be executed. The grisliest, grossest act I could ever conceive had actually happened, and the clearing I had once seen ahead of me disappeared. The change in my course was permanent, my life darkened forever, and the damage irreparable.

If it were Rich, like they said, this was the first picture I'd seen of him in so long, and now maybe the last I'd ever see. I had to be certain it was him, so I watched the video over and over for days, studying the dangling, inert body as it made each slow turn. Every time the camera caught the face, I looked for something that I recognized, anything that told me it was Rich, because unless someone could say to me with absolute certainty that the man on the videotape was my husband and that he was indeed dead, hope would never die. If it were possible that it might not be him, then I had to keep faith alive — faith in Rich, in myself, and in my belief that he would come home to us. I wasn't going to let go of even the slightest of chances that he was still living.

I didn't want anyone else to, either. I tried to explain that if I couldn't discern my own husband from the man on the tape, how was anyone else going to decide if it were really him? I wanted the government and the U.N. to keep in mind that it might be another hoax, another way to scare the U.S. so that we would pressure Israel to release Sheik Obeid. I wasn't going to truly believe that it was Rich until we had proof. I needed some definite confirmation he had been murdered, not just a horribly doctored terrorists' video.

Besides, the tape was poor quality, gritty and blurry, and I couldn't see the face well enough to say for certain if it were him. I saw what the whole world saw — a man hanging from a makeshift gallows, his hands tied behind his back, his feet bound — completely helpless.

But what I didn't tell anyone, because I didn't want anyone to give up for even a minute, was that the man was Rich. I could tell by his bare feet and by the point in his nose. I could almost make out that unmistakable vein in his forehead. Part of me knew it was Rich, but denied it. Another part knew it, but looked for hidden strings, the hidden stool he was standing on, the "lights-camera-action" of the producer. I told no one.

I was glad for the spottiness of the film. The tape was horrifying enough as it was, and I didn't need to see its images in color or close-up shots. My imagination filled in all those gaps; the piercing sounds of agony and abuse, the heavy pall of absolute fear, the air infected with the rabid odor of hate. Every second of what had happened before the execution was etched into my mind, and I felt what the rest of the country could not. I knew the smells, the sounds, and the pain that were hidden behind the silent footage. They were more than I could bear.

Expert forensic analysts, some from the FBI and CIA, other professionals from around the country, were brought in to answer the questions of authenticity. After extensive examinations, they would be able to determine whether or not it was Rich. I gave them pictures: Rich standing in that position, Rich in a side view, Rich in a closeup. Going through my now yellowing photo albums was my last quest to save him.

In the meantime, I issued a statement to respond to both the tape and the media flurry that had erupted around it. Once again calling themselves the Organization of the Oppressed on Earth, the terrorists declared that because "criminal America and the Zionist enemy" did not release Obeid, Colonel Higgins had been killed. His execution was intended to be "an example for those who fear the day of reckoning."

In my own statement, I said that I was aware of the videotape, had seen it, and couldn't draw any conclusions from it myself. All reports of Rich's death were still unconfirmed, but I was preparing for the worst. I told the public that over the past 17 months, I learned that the truth is hard to find and still remained so. However, I was determined to know the truth, and the rest of the country should be, as well, including the U.S. government.

In Washington, they were finally shocked and infuriated enough to deal head on with the hostage issue. On August 1st, the day after the tape was released, officials from the White House to the Pentagon began scrambling for answers, reasons, and a way to respond to the terrorists' actions.

President Bush, on a trip to the Midwest, returned to the White House immediately after the story broke. He said he, like all of America, was shocked right down to the core, and I believed he was truly shaken by what Hezbollah had done. "There is no way that I can properly express the outrage that I feel," he said. President Bush had always been a champion of Rich and of my struggle to have him released, so I knew that now, when it mattered most, his concern was sincere.

He wasn't just doing his job as President. His impassioned pleas for a return to decency and honor were framed by a frank outrage. There was an urgency in his voice, an anger that told me that when he denounced what had happened, he meant it.

President Bush was visibly distressed as well, cameras catching only quick glimpses of him after his speeches as he hurried off to the Cabinet Room for meetings with national security advisors.

Policy makers took the same stance as the President, and the Senate unanimously gave him carte blanche for an "appropriate response," but what was an "appropriate response"? Hezbollah had just killed one of our best military men. How do we react?

In Washington, there was a lot of support for a military response rather than a diplomatic one. A military strike would not only be felt by the hostage takers, but it would also send a warning against further kidnapping. When the administration began accelerating military planning, the idea of an attack seemed like a reality. Naval forces moved within striking distance of terrorist centers in Lebanon and Iran. Also, the administration was considering a sequence of military actions that would systematically increase the pressure on radical groups like Hezbollah.

It was up to President Bush whether or not to go ahead with the military endeavor. I wanted him to fight back, to channel the animosity I heard in his voice into action. But there were other conditions he had to weigh into the problem, like the risk of terrorists responding to any U.S. military action by kidnapping other Americans or executing those they already held.

Also, where exactly were Rich's captors? President Bush couldn't approve a plan whereby the U.S. military hit another country without knowing precisely where the enemy was located. Innocent people might be killed. I understood the President's dilemma, but hadn't Rich been one of the innocent people, too?

It seemed to me that with Sheik Obeid in the hands of the Israelis, he could be forced to give information about the whereabouts of Hezbollah. Media reports said he had already confessed during interrogations to a role in Rich's capture. I believed from the bottom of my heart he had been involved in every aspect of Rich's capture, from the planning to guiding to Rich's eventual transfer to Beirut.

The possibility of an attack coupled with the release of the tape consumed the nation. The tape played again and again on CNN, and shots of it were plastered on the front page of every major newspaper. Seventy-five million television viewers and everyone that read a morning paper saw my husband swinging from the gallows.

People I had never met around the country were watching my husband die while they had their morning coffee and ate breakfast. Did they stop long enough to wonder what kind of man Rich was, what he had done for his country, for the U.N., for them? Did they understand what the video did to me and the rest of our family? Did they know that every time I watched it I felt like I was being cut in two, like my spirit had been severed and a part of it discarded? Rich's family wasn't like the rest of the country. We were different because we couldn't turn off the television and make it go away. The horror of it was with us all the time.

And then the worst got worse.

How do I feel? The Commandant came in and gave me the word that the FBI report says it is you and the man in the picture is dead — but not from hanging. These are the experts. This is what I said I would wait for. And it's here. The Commandant does not give up easily. But we are pragmatists. You taught me to be one. I will not give up on you, but changing my public attitude just now may be right. It appears as if you have been murdered.

They murdered you.

I've thought many times about life without you. Would I stay here, in the Marine Corps? Would I sell your Jag or your bike or your truck? How about your clothes or guns, etc.? But living life without you — never having you come home again. Growing old not being married to Rich Higgins. Being a widow. God, Rich, how is it possible?

And your daughter. Here is a girl who at 19 has no father. You will not see her graduate from college. You will not be here to give her away at her wedding.

Did you know when you were being killed that you were dying? How could a man like you, so good, so kind, so wonderful, be killed? You brought good to so many people, but your mission was not over. Your last mission was one of peace. And, with all this wrangling over the hostages maybe this will bring peace to the other hostages and to the people of Lebanon. Lebanon has never been so bad until you were taken. You already have made a difference. But you had to die to make it true.

Damn, Rich, you are wonderful. I want you to be happy, to smile, to see the good that Chrissy and I have done in your name. I hope you are resting and smiling upon us.

I really get my strength from you. I don't want a chaplain, I don't want a friend. I want you and if I have to be alone to have you, I will be alone.

I love you. I always will my whole life. So many good things will happen in your name. You will never be forgotten. You will always stand for strength, courage, and right. Chrissy and I will take our strength from that.

General Al Gray's support was there until the end. The Marine Commandant, Rich's friend for many years, came to tell me personally on August 7th that the analysts concluded the man in the tape was Rich. The experts said it was possible that he died months ago since there was nothing in the tape that indicated the date. This meant that Rich's captors killed him and then possibly kept his dead body for use as a pawn in their twisted diplomacy.

When the Commandant told me the results of the FBI examinations and that Rich's death was confirmed, it was one of the few times I allowed myself tears. I wept for Rich, for myself, for Chrissy, for the world, my knees finally buckling under the weight of the past seventeen months. The Commandant understood. I fell into his strong arms, let them fold around me, and wept.

He knew it was a rare moment for me. I didn't often let my grief go like that, but I couldn't help it. I honestly never believed it would end like that — Rich suddenly dead and never coming back. The idea of life without Rich came only in flashes, moments of terror that I quickly forced out of my head. What I had truly believed, what I lived and prayed for was Rich's return. I had allowed myself rare moments of doubt, but I had always believed he would come home alive.

Why did I now need to accept that he was dead? Why now and not six months ago? Why couldn't I keep hoping that until Rich was returned, he might be alive?

It was hard to admit that I would never see Rich again. I wanted so badly to refuse that he was gone, to deny that he would never be in our house or share our bed with me or be a father ever again.

But I couldn't live in a dream world. I couldn't go on insisting that Rich was alive and not even possibly dead while forensic experts and national leaders were confirming his death. I had to face the facts, endure the sharp, cruel edges of my reality. I was a widow now, and a life that I never imagined for myself lay ahead.

It began on August 8th when I held a press conference at the Pentagon. I wanted to do this publicly. I didn't want to hide anymore. Mr. Howard and my colleagues rushed to set it up. As I was ushered to the podium, the one I had prepared Mr. Howard so many times to step up to, there must have been a hundred cameras. But I didn't see any of them. I saw Rich. And this is what I said:

> *Yesterday afternoon, the Commandant of the Marine Corps, General Gray, advised me of the virtual certainty that my husband, Colonel Rich Higgins, is dead. Shortly thereafter, I received a telephone call from the President, who graciously offered his support and sympathy.*

*Rich went to Lebanon in the service of the United
Nations because he believed he could be useful, that he
could help, and that he was needed. He always had a
need to fulfill his destiny, a need based on a profound
sense of duty. He wrote in his high school yearbook his
goal was "to always make my family proud of me."*

*Those of us who have known Rich Higgins count
ourselves lucky. He taught us how to love and enjoy life.
He taught us tolerance for those whose ideas differed
from ours. He taught us that words such as honor,
reputation, integrity, and fidelity have real meaning. To
those who would suggest that our concern for Rich should
somehow be mitigated because he was in a dangerous
business or because his act of volunteering was supposedly
foolish, Rich himself would have the appropriate reply:
"When you're out front, people will shoot at you."*

This time, I wasn't just confronting my worst fears. I was
confirming them, in public, and I wanted that public to know the kind of
man that Rich was. I told them about his honor, integrity, and fidelity; he
was the living definition of all three and made those of us around him
better people.

I also recognized the support that both the President and the
Commandant had extended to me and the rest of Rich's family. Each
man had publicly agonized in a very profound and personal way over
Rich's fate. I wanted America to know that both men had been there for
me, as leaders, advisors, supporters, and sympathizers.

President Bush also made another statement after the examinations
concluded. He angrily denounced the murder, but wouldn't commit to a
military response. Our forces were ready, but we continued to effect our
"business-as-usual" policy. At that moment, they were again threatening
the life of another American, Joseph Ciccipio. And our response: If they
harm Ciccipio, we will act. But not for one man, not for Rich. President
Bush's hands were tied. I tried to understand that, but it was, nonetheless,
hard to accept that Rich's murder wasn't worth immediate retaliation.

At least President Bush and the U.S. government tried to fight for
Rich. The U.N., on the other hand, was not so willing to stand up for

him. Marrack Goulding, U.N. Undersecretary for Special Political Affairs, had been attending to other business when the tape of Rich was released. Unlike President Bush, he didn't feel compelled to interrupt his mission to address the issue of the tape. The Secretary General had his office issue a statement, but that was it. There was a brief, unproductive meeting between de Cuellar and me on August 2nd and then a call from a U.N. official — not from de Cuellar or Goulding personally — on August 9th informing me that Goulding, like everyone else, was concluding that Rich was dead.

Even after the murder was confirmed, there was little response from Goulding or the U.N. and certainly no action. They had neglected Rich's capture before, but this was a new low. Now they had completely forgotten him. We sent the U.N. a healthy Marine, and what did they do with him? They abandoned him on the battlefield.

Even if Rich was dead, I couldn't let go of him. I wouldn't leave him alone the way that the U.N. had. We were still connected, and although I might never see him again, he would always be with me. While he was held hostage, I didn't know where he was, who had him, and what they were doing to him. There was never any physical contact during those seventeen months, no letters exchanged, no phone calls, or even a message.

Still, Rich and I were not wholly separated. We always had more than a physical connection, drawn together by emotion and spirit. Without any tangible forms of contact, I still communed with Rich. My journal kept our link alive. Every night when I sat down to write, it was my time with Rich. I didn't know where or how he was in body, but I knew that his spirit was strong, reaching out for me, knowing that I would be there.

So, I couldn't stop writing to him now. Even if he were dead, he weren't home, and I didn't know where he was. Some part of Rich, whatever it was — his spirit, his legacy, his mission — would always be out there. I needed to stay in touch with that, to bring him home to rest peacefully. Writing to him was a way to bind me to Rich until whatever physical part of him remained in this world was returned.

I didn't know when that would happen. The shock of Rich's murder was still fresh, for both me and the Bush administration. At the same time that Hezbollah released the videotape, they also threatened to kill remaining American hostages, and the U.S. government had to watch as closely as possible the terrorists' every move.

I knew that the focus was shifting from Rich to the other hostages. It was imperative that the government prevent the loss of another American if they could. At the same time, I needed an explanation, some concrete information about Rich's death. Knowing the facts was the only way I would ever be able to finally accept his death. Without proof, there would be no closure.

The unanswered questions, the ones I needed to resolve before I could move on, rose before me like a mountain. I stood at the bottom, exhausted, but trying to summon the strength to tackle the next climb. I had to know what happened. If Rich didn't die by hanging, how did he die? Where was his body? He deserved to be brought home, laid to rest with honor and dignity. But was anyone even going to look for him?

Chapter 16

March Always in
the Ranks of Honor

Month 18
August 16, 1989

It's hard to write to you now. I want to write; there are still things to tell you. I still feel we are spiritually close, but damn, I miss you so and I'm so sad for you. You wanted so much to do good, to succeed — and to be a good husband and father. And you did, you are — but it looks like we will all live apart forever.

Yesterday the Commandant gave his blessing on a Rich Higgins tribute day. Today Turley is raising money for the fund. Two guys in Texas who hardly know you have collected $20,000 so far.

I just want to be left alone. I don't want to have to make small talk. I don't want to have to smile. I just want to be alone.

I love you.

In the weeks and months that followed the release of the videotape, there was an overflow of support for Rich from the media and the public. I wanted to be left alone, but the rest of the country wanted to know about Rich. They were interested in his mission and his career. Men like the Commandant helped. He took every opportunity given him to keep Rich's legacy alive, as did his fellow Marines.

When Rich was initially captured, the media presented a distorted picture of his character and the circumstances of his abduction. Journalists and reporters developed their own angles on the story, often neglecting to include the facts. Some called him a good Marine, while others said he was a reckless cowboy. They labeled him as an earnest peacekeeper one minute and a blatant rule-breaker the next. The opportunity to sensationalize Rich's personality, his career, and his kidnapping was too hard for certain media types to pass up. As a result, newspaper and magazine readers and the television viewers, too, knew neither what kind of man Rich really was nor what actually happened to him.

This new barrage of media attention was different. Newspapers and publications that ran the gamut from *The Washington Post* to the *Marine Corps Gazette* to *Ladies Home Journal* printed stories about Rich. This time they used words like "honor," "dignity," and "integrity" to describe him. They said he was the epitome of what the Marine Corps stood for. America was finally getting to know the same Rich Higgins that his friends and family had known all along; the man who was willing to save others before himself, even if it meant risking his life.

Like the two men in Texas who only knew Rich from having gone through Marine Corps training with him in 1967, people were affected by what they read and saw on television, and they responded, voicing their shock and disgust. Their anger was heard in the dozens of editorials from around the country that denounced his murder. Rich's death struck a nerve with the American people, and they were crying out in protest. An article in the *Woodbridge Weekly Messenger*, our hometown in Virginia, summed up the public sentiment better than any when it said: "As our own outrage ebbs with time, a passage from the book *Sophie's Choice* comes to mind. After surviving the horrors of a concentration camp during World War II, the woman says the worst of it was not the deprivation and institutionalized cruelty, but the fact the people came to accept it. This is the real threat — that we will learn to live with madmen, yield to them, perhaps not even noticing what we have lost."[28]

Finally the country was grasping the severity of the hostage situation. They were understanding the utter irrationality of it all and beginning to see that Rich had died at the hands of madmen simply because he was working for peace.

Terrorists had indiscriminately killed another American citizen, and it was no longer acceptable. America was refusing to sit back and live with it. People wanted to know why, how, and where Rich died.

They were questions that consumed me, too. The not knowing was the most torturous part of the whole ordeal. The paucity of information, the inability to find Rich, all of it was wearing me down. There were so many days when I felt ready to just give in, to surrender to the agony and the sorrow that racked my mind. The terrorists who had captured Rich were finally going to beat me because I didn't know how much longer I could endure the torment of my unanswered questions, my unresolved emotions. Hezbollah's sick games of cat-and-mouse, their unwillingness to cooperate in any way, was harder than ever to stomach.

They had murdered Rich, and in doing so, weakened me. Now they were refusing me one last chance to say goodbye, and until I had that chance, there would be no finality. I would run myself into the ground searching for him.

As the weeks became months and there were still no facts about Rich's death, I began to doubt that we would ever be able to bury him in American soil. I wasn't ever sure what the U.S. or the U.N. was doing to answer all of the questions surrounding his murder, but if they were using the same plan of attack as before, Rich would never be found. If the posturing and lip service that I had seen and heard since February 17, 1988, continued, I would never get the resolution I needed to put all this behind me.

By October, I had decided that, once again, nothing would happen unless I made it. I began my second campaign to get Rich home, knowing this time I was asking only for his remains. On October 21, 1989, I made

---

[28] Woodbridge *Weekly Messenger*, "Outrage Ebbs," August 2, 1989.

my first official plea to Secretary General de Cuellar. I explained that abandoning Rich now would be a heinous crime. The U.N. owed him the dignity of retrieving his body. Again, I compared Rich's situation to abandoning the dead on the battlefield. No honorable soldier would consider it, but was the U.N. an honorable soldier?

I didn't hear from de Cuellar or anyone in his office for nearly two months. It wasn't until December 7th that I even received a reply. I knew then that the U.N., as before, was doing nothing for Rich.

I turned to our government. Shortly before Christmas of 1989, I wrote to President Bush. Nine senators (John McCain, Steve Symms, Trent Lott, Nancy Landon Kassebaum, John Warner, John Glenn, Slade Gorton, Strom Thurmond, and Sam Nunn) also wrote and signed a letter urging the President to impress upon the U.N. that the U.S. would not stand by and allow a member of our military to be abandoned. If the U.S. was to continue to support peacekeeping efforts, the U.N. must take responsibility for the men and women the U.S. sends them. Also, we asked the President to insist that a member of the Secretary General's staff be assigned to pursue Rich's case on a full-time basis.

Because the public had rallied so around Rich, I took my cause to the people. I wasn't appearing on talk shows every week or giving interviews to every reporter who asked, but I wasn't as publicity shy as before, either. I granted interviews to journalists and reporters who would support my cause. I talked to the ones who understood that, dead or alive, I still wanted to bring Rich home.

I also began public speaking with engagements at events like the U.N. Staff Union Human Rights Program. I told the crowds that innocent men like Rich could not continue to be fodder for political dreams. If the U.N. had aspirations for peace and were willing to let men and women put their lives at risk to achieve it, then they must stand behind those men and women. I wanted my speeches to really hit home, to make my audience think about what had happened to Rich and what could happen to other peacekeepers.

If my speeches were going to make an impression, they needed to vex the public conscience, let them know what had been done and what had not, what could have been done and what actually happened. At the same time, I had to speak to their hearts, make them understand just some of the emotions that a hostage family feels. I used sayings and verses like "blessed are the peacemakers for they shall be called the children of God," and I knew that those words would stay with them. Anyone who heard me would not soon forget Rich Higgins.

Speaking and writing about him helped me to feel less alone. When I looked out over a crowd or thought of readers lingering over an editorial I had gotten published, I felt the support and concern of the people. To know that so many were behind me and believed in what Rich had done, was a source of great strength and a tremendous consolation. It eased my anger, helping me to channel it into something good. The energy that might be exhausted by my frustration was turned toward positive endeavors. And speaking and writing were a constant reminder of the values Rich taught me — moral and physical courage, integrity, and compassion. Every time I wrote his story or mentioned his name, those lessons were internalized anew.

I spent the rest of 1989 and all of 1990 on my "Remember Rich" campaign. The more time that went by, the more likely it was that people, including the U.N. and the U.S. government, would forget him. So it was my responsibility to keep Rich in the minds and hearts of not just the public, but U.S. and U.N. officials as well. I couldn't stop telling people our story.

On July 6, 1990, Rich was officially declared dead by the Marine Corps. Even when the Commandant made the official report, I wouldn't give up. The Commandant had yet to make a conclusive report since the only significant evidence of Rich's murder was the video. Until now, he had been listed as missing and captured, and the Commandant had been waiting to see if a body would be recovered. He wanted to make sure beyond a shadow of a doubt that Rich was dead, but by July of 1990 too much time had passed without any evidence to indicate otherwise.

I tried not to let it set me back. General Al Gray had always been one of our strongest supporters. I knew he would only do something like that if it was absolutely necessary. He had waited as long as he could to do what we all knew had to be done. I knew myself that Rich was gone, but it was hard to let go completely, hard to watch his death become "official" in the minds of his Marines. As I read the death certificate, DD Form 1300, I knew that now Rich was another casualty statistic. Just the bare facts of his life were there; date of birth, race, sex, religious preference, duty status were the among the only things that went on the report. His date and place of death were listed as "not known."

After the Commandant's report, we held a memorial service for Rich at Quantico National Cemetery. It was not a funeral. I wouldn't have one until we had his remains, but it was a chance to honor Rich in a way we hadn't before. We dedicated a spot on Memorial Walk to him with a plaque that reads, *Qui procol hinc, qui ante diem perrit: Sed miles, sed pro patria.* "He died far away, before his time, but as a soldier and for his country."

The memorial renewed any faith I'd lost with the filing of the report. Taking time to remember Rich fueled my desire to see him returned to the States for a proper burial. He deserved it, and I wouldn't stop until it happened. The next few months and on into 1991 were spent doing more speaking, writing, and fighting for Rich.

Another winter and spring passed, and by 1991, American hostages in Lebanon were slowly being freed. I rejoiced as each man was released, but I grieved over my own loss. I avoided reading the newspaper accounts and watching the television reports of the returned hostages and their families. I tried to share in their joy, but I knew that kind of happiness would never come to me. I would never see Rich step from a plane, so elated to be on American soil that he fell to his knees and then into my arms. That would never happen, and each man who returned was another reminder that I didn't know where my husband was.

I kept telling America that there were still hostages in the Middle East. People couldn't forget the families that were not sharing in the homecoming joy. I wouldn't and couldn't ever forget what the terrorists had done. The filthy hostage fabric had spit out the bones of my husband, and if we forgave them, if we forgot what they did, if we thanked these savages simply because they released some unharmed, then we were merely inviting them at a time and place they would select, to kill again. Shame on us if we did.

In the summer of 1991, talk of releasing the remaining American hostages was on the table. In return for freeing hostages, the kidnappers wanted immunity and protection, which made the U.S. wary of the deal.

If any negotiations were going to turn into reliable agreements to return the Americans, I felt as though Rich's name should be on the list.

I spent months lobbying for that to happen. One by one, each man returned to his family, and by December 2, 1991, the last of the remaining hostages, Terry Anderson, came home. Secretary General de Cuellar assured me that by the end of the year, Rich's body would be in the U.S., too.

I had trouble believing that. Now that all the American hostages had been returned, would the U.N. really work toward bringing the only dead man home? They had done so little for Rich when he was alive, why would they do anything for him now? My only ray of hope rested in the fact that the Secretary General was nearing the end of his term at the U.N. If he wanted to leave on a positive note, if he wanted to appear to have "solved" the hostage problem, then he would make sure everyone was home, including Rich.

Since Terry Anderson had finally been released, there was no danger that anything I said or did would endanger an American hostage. For nearly four years, I had been hesitant to say or do too much for fear that it would put Rich and the others at risk. If I angered the kidnappers, then they would take it out on the hostages. If I spoke harshly against the government, they wouldn't work with me at all.

Now, however, there was no one to harm; all the Americans were home, and Rich had been murdered. On December 3rd, *The New York Times* published another editorial piece that I'd written. This time my pen leaked venom. I was bitter, and America was going to know why. I told them that the State Department and the U.N. had treated me with deference and politeness and then ignored me. They assumed that since I was military, I wouldn't speak out against them. I would be loyal to the system, and they were right. They had known all along how to manipulate me.

I wrote that I believed a decision was made early on not to give even the appearance of doing anything different for Rich. To do something different for a military man than for a civilian would be politically unwise and might cause a furor by certain influential civilian and media types. I ended the editorial by writing what Rich had always told me: Those who wear the uniform of their country go into harm's way because they know

America will come after them when they go down. Sometime between February 17, 1988, and July 31, 1989, Rich learned that was not true.

Despite my public disappointment in the U.N., the Secretary General continued to assure me that Rich would be returned before the new year. De Cuellar, U.N. spokesman Timor Goksell, and U.N. hostage negotiator Giandomenico Picco were said to be working on the release of his remains, and for the first time, their negotiations yielded results for me.

On December 22, 1991, an anonymous caller notified the American University Hospital that a body had been dumped along the side of a Beirut road. When the partially decomposed body was delivered to the hospital morgue it had been, according to Lebanon's coroner-general Ahmed Harati, wrapped in cotton and bandages in a poor attempt to embalm it. Even before extensive examination, Harati seemed reasonably sure it was Rich. The hair still on the head was in a crew cut, the facial features were those of a Westerner, and there were black marks around the neck.

The next day, after two examinations, Dr. Harati and U.N. and U.S. officials confirmed that the body was Rich. It was December 23rd, my 41st birthday and our 14th wedding anniversary. On the same day that Rich had married me, he was coming home to me in a flag-draped casket.

His body was driven immediately from the morgue in an escorted ambulance and taken to the embassy in the east Beirut suburb of Aukar. Finally, Rich was safe, blanketed by an American flag and protected by the armed guards who stood watch at the embassy's hilltop compound. He was to be flown from Beirut to Dover Air Force Base in Delaware, where the Marine Corps would receive the body, and then on to Andrews Air Force Base.

I decided that I would say very little about Rich's return. The U.S. and the U.N. were still working on the release of another murdered hostage's remains, CIA Station Chief William Buckley, who was killed in 1985. I didn't want to hinder their efforts, so I made only a general statement about the return of Rich's remains. I told the public that I was relieved to see that this tragic situation seemed to be moving to a conclusion. It had been almost four years for our family, and the waiting was finally ending. But it was not the end that we spent years hoping for.

On December 24th, I went on the three morning network television shows, once again speaking about my husband's return, but this time knowing that he would come home in a coffin. Each interviewer asked me if I felt relieved in any way. It had been so long since there was any relief in my life. I wasn't sure that I would recognize the feeling, but I told them that this was what our family needed. We had to see Rich put to rest here so that there would be some respite from the nightmare, some closure to the last four years.

At NBC, CBS, and ABC, they all asked another tough question. They wanted to know how I felt about the kidnappers. Did I believe they should get protection? Freedom from retribution? Naturally, I had thought about what should happen to the kidnappers before, but, realistically, I never considered that the U.S. or the U.N. would ever be in a position to actually dictate a punishment or non-punishment to them.

I told the interviewers that "there's got to be someone that's greater than us that will judge a man who kidnaps, tortures, and murders an unarmed U.N. peacekeeper. The person who will hang the body on videotape for his daughter, his wife, and his family to watch and then dump it on a street in Beirut has to, one day, meet with a greater force that will judge what has been done. And if I have to, I'm willing to wait for that judgment."

The truth is I wanted them dead, I wanted them hanging by a noose for the world to see, I wanted to hear the wailing of their children. But it wasn't in me to say that, it wasn't the right time or place. My only job now was to see that their disgracing of him ended. When Rich arrived at Dover Air Force Base, he would be in the loving hands of his family and his Marines, and we would treat him with the respect that had been denied him for so long. On Christmas Day, I went to Dover to be alone with the casket; it was not possible to see what was left of him. In keeping with Corps' tradition, a Marine sat with the body, and our good friend, Brigadier General Tom Draude gave up his Christmas to stay with Rich. There was nothing these Marine officers wouldn't do for one another.

The depth of the military bond went farther than the constant vigil at Dover. Five days later, on December 30th, the remains of both Rich and William Buckley arrived at Andrews Air Force Base, and an interment ceremony was held for both men. Their coffins were carried from C-41 transport planes by Marine pallbearers in dress blues. A red-jacketed Marine band played Lee Greenwood's "God Bless the U.S.A." as Rich's coffin was brought down the ramp. I sat with my head bowed while Navy chaplain Larry Ellis prayed over both men, calling them "not fallen soldiers, not victims, but heroic servants of freedom."

When I looked up, the coffin stared back at me in silence. I was sitting in the front row, and Rich was closer to me than he had been in nearly four years, close enough to walk to him, to reach out and grab him, but there was no man to touch. There was only the long, shiny, silver box that held his remains.

I wore my dress blue uniform as Rich would have wanted me to. I felt the cold, gray wind blow right through me and watched it rustle the edges of the flag hanging down the sides of Rich's coffin. Did he feel the cold I felt? The lonely, desolate cold that made my body want to shake? I didn't even let myself shiver for fear that feeling too much of anything, even if it were the wind, would open the flood gates of emotion. And I wouldn't fall apart, not here, not when Rich needed me to be more than his wife, not when he needed me to be a Marine.

As friends and family of Rich and Buckley listened, Secretary of Defense Richard Cheney, Vice President Dan Quayle, and CIA Director Robert Gates commended the two men for their bravery, patriotism, and their ultimate sacrifice. They told us that America owed them a debt of gratitude that we can never repay. They had given their lives in the pursuit of peace and freedom. In Quayle's speech, he said something that has stayed with me. He said that Rich was more of a free man, even in captivity, than his murderers would ever be. I believe it's true.

I decided not to have Rich buried at Arlington like William Buckley, but at Quantico National Cemetery instead. Quantico had always been a special place for Rich. It was where Rich started his career in the Marines and where we met more than fifteen years before. I thought it only fitting that he should end it there as well.

The Corps planned a full honors burial service for Rich, which was normally a ceremony reserved only for a general officer. The hearse carrying the coffin was preceded by the Marine Band and a company from Eighth and I Barracks, the Marines' showcase unit in Washington. Three hundred American flags lined the road leading to the grave site, looking bright and new against the bleak winter sky. The sounds of them snapping in the stiff breeze accompanied the low echo of the Marine Band drums. We could hear their rhythmic thumps rolling through the cemetery a full ten minutes before the procession came into view.

As the honor guard lifted Rich's silver coffin from the hearse, the band played "The Marines' Hymn," and I stood at attention, saluting the Marine who had served for over 20 years and the man I had known for 15.

There were over two hundred people at Quantico to pay respects to Rich, including General Colin Powell and Senator Bob Dole. They heard the Reverend Howard Olds, a minister from Louisville, praise Rich as a husband, father, a soldier, and a peacekeeper. While Rev. Olds spoke, the Marine band stood behind him playing "The Impossible Dream." I chose that song because it was so apt for Rich and for his lifelong battle, always dreaming the patriot's dream of peace and freedom, and finally, scorned and covered with scars, with his last ounce of courage, still striving for what was, indeed, an impossible dream. I realized that I, too, shared that impossible patriot's dream with him — and always would.

Much of the family became emotional during the service, but I knew that I had to steady myself again against the tide of emotions welling up inside. I couldn't let anything go during the ceremony. If I started, I don't know if I could have stopped. Instead, I rose from my seat, went forward, and knelt beside Rich. I bowed my head, feeling the cold steeliness of the coffin, knowing that Rich was inside, resting finally. I tried to stretch my arms as far around that steel as possible before I said goodbye.

As the service was ending, the honor guard lifted the flag from the coffin, folded it, and gave it to the Commandant. Gen. Carl E. Mundy gave one, a special pre-folded flag to 21-year-old Chrissy. He knelt and laid his hands on mine, and while whispering the age-old words "on behalf of a grateful Nation," he gave the other to me.

While Marine riflemen took aim and fired into the sky, Rich was lowered into the ground.

Lieutenant Colonel Rich Higgins Arrival Ceremony
Andrews Air Force Base, Maryland
December 30, 1991

Chapter 17

At Rest, But Not at Peace

Laying Rich to rest finally gave some semblance of closure to an agonizing, incomprehensible period of my life. The pain, however, did not end, neither did the anger, the sorrow, or the heartbreak. Those, I fear, will never fully subside.

Having Rich buried on American soil did restore the freedom that was taken from him when terrorists captured him on that roadside in south Lebanon. Over the next four years, they would continue to dishonor him, in life and in death, stripping a once- proud Marine of any human decency.

What exactly Rich went through is something I'll never know and probably never completely understand. What I do know is that it must never happen again. After Rich was returned to us and buried at Quantico, it became my personal and professional mission to see that Rich's fate was never visited upon another member of the U.S. military, and that no other family had to suffer like ours did.

Since 1991, I've lobbied in Washington for harsher penalties for terrorists and worked toward making people aware of the fact that the U.N. will never be fully able to protect Americans under its command. I've written to and spoken with congressmen and U.N. officials, pleading for them to help to implement better methods of protecting peacekeepers like Rich. In 1995, I spoke before both the House and the Senate during hearings on the Peace Powers Act and terrorism, respectively. Each time I told them that the U.S. should not send peacekeepers anywhere unless there is first peace to keep. I also told them that if and when terrorism strikes, there must be policies of swift public retribution. That is the only way we can begin to deter these crimes, and that is the only way we can honor our men and women in uniform.

In 1993, I met with Israeli Prime Minister Yitzhak Rabin, the late prime minister, in Israel to thank him for his devotion to Israel's service people, and his willingness to work tirelessly for their release, even and often at the cost of international condemnation. I am forever grateful that I was able to tell him this before he himself was gunned down by a madman.

Three years later, in 1996, I stood on the podium as President Bill Clinton signed into law the Antiterrorism and Effective Death Penalty Act, which established stricter penalties for terrorism and better methods by which the U.S. can combat it.

But for every triumph, there have been countless setbacks and disappointments. I submitted a Freedom of Information Act request that yielded no records of an official investigation ever undertaken by the U.S or the U.N. My letters to Washington went unanswered, and my phone calls were not returned. Slowly the important contacts that I once had dwindled to only one. It was only when I went public with my disappointment in our government that I elicited a response from anyone. Even then, officials were apathetic in their replies to my questions and suggestions concerning finding Rich's murderers and combating terrorism.

Now, more than ten years after Rich was captured, I know that my questions will never be answered and my pleadings for tough and effective policy to fight terrorism and to protect our servicemen and women may never be heard. Because of that, I will never have any lasting peace. I will never go through one day without being reminded that while my husband endured the unimaginable, his country and the U.N. did nothing. Because of their unwillingness to act, my hands were tied, and I could not do anything to bring my husband home.

People ask me all the time how I survived the horror of losing my husband and the frustration of being incapable of helping him. They ask me how I can go on, and I tell them that my life has gone on since the day

Rich was taken and will continue regardless. But I cannot completely leave this chapter of my life behind. It has become a part of me, and no matter what the future holds, it will continue to be a part of my life. Sometimes it will be in the forefront. Sometimes it will be in the background, but I will continue to live the way I have for the last ten years: to be responsible, to behave in a dignified manner, and to cope the best I can with what fate has offered me.

People have told me that they don't think they could do the same. I don't believe that. I remember remarking to Rich all the time that I was so glad that I didn't know him while he was fighting in Vietnam, that I admired women who went through it with their husbands. I told him that I couldn't have put up with the strain. But then, ironically, I did, and I continue to bear the heavy weight of losing the man whom I loved to senseless, animal violence.

Whether we like it or not, the men and women of the Marine Corps are in a business filled with adversity. Fighting wars and keeping peace is the most difficult and demanding of jobs. I feel lucky. I knew that. As a Marine myself, I understood and accepted the risks of Rich's position. I had the same duty to Corps and country as my husband, and I knew that it would put one or both of us in harm's way at some time in our lives. It was our sworn duty.

I never thought that duty, however, would take Rich away from me forever, yet I don't regret helping Rich make the decision to take the position with the U.N. Still, I continue to feel responsible. I continue to hold myself accountable for Rich's fate. Was there something else I could have done? Another avenue I could have taken? Another lead I could have pursued? My mission to bring Rich home alive was a failure, and while it might have been out of my control, I can't help but feel somewhat responsible. Years of Marine training have taught me that it's not merely the mission that's important, it's the success of the mission that matters. Mine was as tragically unsuccessful as it could be.

The Marine Corps also teaches leadership traits and principles. Many years ago I thought that these were just buzzwords we had to memorize. They are not. They are, without a doubt, real, and because of Rich, I understand how true they are. Words like *integrity, knowledge, courage, decisiveness, dependability, initiative, tact, justice, enthusiasm, bearing, endurance, unselfishness, loyalty*, and *judgment* all have a deep and abiding meaning for me, as a Marine and as a person. Because they make me think of Rich, the words give me strength. They are a part of his legacy and his spirit, and they help me to go on.

People say they admire me, and I have to admit that it feels good to hear that those that I respect feel I have done right. But I don't feel I have done anything special. I certainly didn't choose to be in the position in which I find myself, and I have done nothing but survive as best I can. If, by acting the way that I know Rich would have been proud, I have helped others survive their own trauma or learn to cope with unforeseeable tragedy, then some good will have come of all this. Rich's life will have made a difference.

He was the best Marine officer I ever knew. Rich was a leader. He took charge, took control, and never surrendered, even when he was out front, even when they were shooting at him. When the Navy announced in 1994 that it planned to honor Rich by commissioning a guided missile destroyer in his name, I could think of no finer way to preserve his memory. Even if Rich went forgotten by the government, the U.N., and even the public, he would be forever immortalized by the *USS HIGGINS* and by the men and women who will proudly serve aboard her. Like Rich, she will lead the charge, never backing down, always fighting for what we believe in.

In October 1997, I christened the destroyer *HIGGINS* and watched as it slid into the Kennebec River in Bath, Maine, the beginning of a journey toward unknown shores, toward danger, toward its destiny. I thought of Rich, leaving for the position in the Middle East, going toward the same unknown, the same danger, but at the same time making steps toward the peace that he died for.

In my reverie on that cold day in Maine, Virginia Senator Charles S. Robb said, "The *USS HIGGINS* will put the world on notice: Those who threaten America's interests or dare to terrorize its citizens will face Colonel Rich Higgins and the 8,300 tons of pure American steel that now surround his spirit."

I thought then of the Churchill quotes that I came across so very long ago, right after Rich had been captured: about courage being lonely and the greatest of all human virtues. The words seemed meant for the man who we were remembering today and for the legacy that he left behind. And I silently read in the launch program the words I had them include from Yom Kippur's Kol Nidre service, one of the most solemn of the Jewish year:

> *O source of mercy, give us the grace to show forbearance to those who offend against us. When the wrongs and injustices of others wound us, may our hearts not despair of human good. May no trial, however severe, embitter our souls and destroy our trust. When beset by trouble and sorrow, our mothers and fathers put on the armor of faith and fortitude. May we too find strength to meet adversity with quiet courage and unshaken will. Help us to understand that injustices and hate will not forever afflict the human race; that righteousness and mercy will triumph in the end.[29]*

---

[29] Central Conference of American Rabbis, Rabbi Chaim Stern, ed., *Gates of Repentance: The New Union Prayerbook for the Days of Awe*, 1978, p. 265.

USS Higgins on patrol

Epilogue

After Rich's murder, his friends, coworkers, and acquaintances told me many stories about the kind of man he was. But perhaps one of the most poignant statements about him was one that I uncovered , one that he wrote himself long before he knew how his life would end. It was certainly how he lived; it was no doubt how he died.

In every battle and skirmish since the birth of our Corps, Marines have acquitted themselves with the greatest distinction, winning new honors on each occasion until the term 'Marine' has come to signify all that is highest in military efficiency and soldierly virtue.

John A. Lejeune,Commandant of the Marine Corps

My Credo
Air Command and Staff College,
Montgomery, Alabama September 1979
by Major William R. Higgins

I believe in one Nation under God, indivisible, with liberty and justice for all. I have dedicated my life to the service of my country and have pledged my patriotism, valor, fidelity, and abilities to the people of the United States of America. In return, the President of the United States has vested special trust and confidence in me and has given me the privilege of serving as the defender of my country as a United States Marine. I hold no ambition above service to my God, my Country, and my Corps.

No day holds more meaning in my life than the day when my drill instructor stood in the rain and mud at Quantico, Virginia, looked me square in the eye, and called me "Marine." He initiated me into the brotherhood of the Corps and challenged me to become a leader of men as a professional Marine officer. He promised me a hard pack, a hard time, and a rifle. He delivered that promise, but he delivered much more. He challenged me to be professional to subordinate myself to the institutional demands of the profession of arms. He challenged me, first and foremost, to accomplish the mission and to look always to the welfare of my young Marines. He cautioned me that, to be professional every day of my life, I would have to give more to the Corps than the Corps could give to me. On that day, I began to search for a credo that would serve me and my Marines in peace and war.

As an officer of Marines, I believe it is my charge to set the example. I must create a favorable impression in courage, appearance, and personal conduct. I must be mentally alert, morally straight, and physically strong. I must uphold the personal and professional credo of "doing what is right — even when no one is looking." My integrity can never be challenged and my character must be unimpeachable. My physical courage must be such that I can face the danger of combat with calmness and firmness, and my moral courage must be equal to fear of criticism I will surely face. As a commander, my loyalty to my superiors and my subordinates must be absolute, and I must strive daily for the qualities of judgment and justice to exercise impartiality and consistency in making sound and timely decisions.

I believe I must be technically and tactically proficient. I must strive unceasingly to accomplish the goals of readiness, training, and quality to accomplish any combat mission. To do this, I seek to know my professional and personal limitations and strive through every source of education and experience to seek self-improvement. I demand the same knowledge of my men and believe it is my responsibility to protect their welfare. I shall be certain in the proper performance of my duties, and I shall expect no less from any one of them. I have the responsibility to train them as a team and to keep them always informed. It is my charge to insure that every task is understood, supervised, and accomplished in order that I might develop a deep and sincere sense of responsibility among my Marines. To insure the welfare of the Corps through victory on the battlefield, I must be mindful to employ my command in accordance with its capabilities. In all cases, I believe I must put my personal responsibility before my personal rights. I can never provide for my comfort at the expense of my mission or my Marines.

I believe it is my professional responsibility to seek always the responsible position and to accept responsibility for my actions. I must always display the initiative to seek out what needs to be done and develop a course of action to accomplish that mission. Neither pain, fatigue, distress, nor hardship can come between me and my mission. I must always be a leader of men — and all that term implies.

That is what I believe — this is my credo. This is the credo of my drill instructor, my Commandant, and my Corps.

I believe...
I believe in my God...
I believe in my Country...
I believe in my Corps
Semper Fidelis

This high name of distinction and soldierly repute we who are Marines today have received from those who preceded us in the Corps. With it we also received from them the eternal spirit which has animated the Corps from generation to generation and has been the distinguishing mark of the Marines of every age. So long as that spirit continues to flourish Marines will be found equal to every emergency in the future as they have been in the past, and the men of our nation will regard us as worthy successors to the long line of illustrious men who have served as 'soldiers of the sea' since the founding of our Corps.

— General John A. Lejeune

A friend, Colonel Fred Peck, poses in front of one of many memorials to slain Colonel Higgins, this one in Bardera, Somalia, Operation Restore Hope, December 1992.

WELCOME TO
HELLGATE PRESS

THE UNEXPECTED STORM

The Gulf War Legacy ISBN: 1-55571-542-7
by Steven Manchester 260 pages, Hardcover: $21.95

After rigorous physical exams, soldiers were trained to fight, infused with rage, and sent to strike—only to watch biology and technology do their jobs for them. Operation Desert Storm was a war like no other. What our troops brought home with them as a result of experimental vaccines, radioactive depleted uranium, and so much pent-up rage, is just beginning to surface. This is one soldier's story.

LIFE IN THE FRENCH FOREIGN LEGION

How to Join and What to Expect When You Get There
by Evan McGorman ISBN: 1-55571-532-X
250 pages, Hardcover: $22.95

Five years is a long time to commit to anything—especially when your life could be at stake. Consider, prepare, and plan before you enlist. *Life in the French Foreign Legion* is based on this insider's account of what life is really like in one the most mysterious military organizations in the world.

PILOTS, MAN YOUR PLANES!

A History of Naval Aviation ISBN: 1-55571-466-8
by Wilbur H. Morrison 474 pages, Hardcover: $33.95

An account of naval aviation from Kitty Hawk to the Gulf War, *Pilots, Man Your Planes!* tells the story of naval air growth from a time when planes were launched from battleships to the major strategic element of naval warfare it is today. This book is filled with rare photographs, detailed maps, and accurate accounts that can be found nowhere else. Ideal for anyone interested in aviation.

ARMY MUSEUMS

West of the Mississippi   ISBN: 1-55571-395-5
by Fred L. Bell, SFC, Retired **318 pages, Paperback: $17.95**

A guide book for travelers through 23 museums of the west. *Army Museums* contains detailed information about the contents of each museum and the famous soldiers stationed at the forts and military reservations where the museums are located. It is a colorful look at our heritage and the settling of the American West.

FROM HIROSHIMA WITH LOVE

by Raymond A. Higgins   ISBN: 1-55571-404-8
      320 pages, Paperback: $18.95

Written from detailed notes and diary entries, *From Hiroshima With Love* is the remarkable story of Lieutenant Commander Wallace Higgins and his experiences in Hiroshima. As Military Governor, Higgins was responsible for helping rebuild a ravaged nation. In doing so, he developed an unforeseen respect for the Japanese, their culture, and one special woman.

WALKING AWAY FROM THE THIRD REICH

The Experiences of a Teenager in Hitler's Army
by Claus W. Sellier   ISBN: 1-55571-513-3
      308 pages, Paperback: $15.95

Seventeen-year-old boys are the same everywhere. This is a gripping story of a well-to-do German boy who is eager to serve, but learns the hard way that war is not a game. From the shelter of his private boys' school, to the devastating battle fields of Germany, he learns what is truly important to him.

TO ORDER OR FOR MORE INFORMATION
1 - 8 0 0 - 2 2 8 - 2 2 7 5 *(telephone)*
i n f o @ p s i - r e s e a r c h . c o m *(email)*
w w w . p s i - r e s e a r c h . c o m *(Website)*

THE WAR THAT WOULD NOT END
U.S. Marines in Vietnam, 1971-1973 ISBN: 1-55571-420-X
by Major Charles D. Melson, USMC (Retired)

388 pages, Paperback: $19.95

When South Vietnamese troops proved unable to take over the war from their American counterparts, the Marines had to resume responsibility. Covering the period 1971-1973, Major Charles D. Melson describes the battle strategies of the units that broke a huge 1972 enemy offensive. The book contains a detailed look at this often ignored period of America's longest war. Featured as an alternate selection in the DoubleDay Book Club.

PROJECT OMEGA
Eye of the Beast ISBN: 1-55571-511-7

by James E. Acre **228 pages, Paperback: $13.95**

"CNN tried its level best to dishonor the reputation of the brave men of Special Operations Group. ... Acre's beautifully written and accurate portrayal of some of the actions of that noble unit will allow the reader to see how these daring young men made accomplishing the impossible routine and to also set the record straight."

— David Hackworth, Author of *About Face and Hazardous Duty*

GULF WAR DEBRIEFING BOOK
An After Action Report ISBN: 1-55571-396-3

by Andrew Leyden **318 pages, Paperback: $18.95**

Available in the George Bush Presidential Library Museum Store. Now you can draw your own conclusion as to what happened during the seven-month period between late 1990 and early 1991. The *Gulf War Debriefing Book: An After Action Report* provides you with a meticulous review of the events. It includes documentation of all military units deployed, the primary weapons used during the war, and a look at the people, places, and politics behind the military maneuvering.

ORDER OF BATTLE

Allied Ground Forces of Operation Desert Storm
by Thomas D. Dinackus   ISBN: 1-55571-493-5
                              407 pages, Paperback: $17.95

Contains photographs of medals, ribbons, and unit patches
Based on extensive research—containing information
not previously available to the public—*Order of Battle:
Allied Ground Forces of Operation Desert Storm* is a
detailed study of the Allied ground combat units that
served in the conflict in the Persian Gulf. In addition to
showing unit assignments, it includes the type of insignia
and equipment used by the various units in one of the
largest military operations since the end of WWII.

GREEN HELL

The Battle for Guadalcanal   ISBN: 1-55571-498-6
by William J. Owens   284 pages, Paperback: $18.95

This is the story of thousands of Melanesian, Australian,
New Zealanders, Japanese, and American men who fought
for a poor insignificant island in a faraway corner of the
South Pacific Ocean. For the men who participated, the real
battle was of man against jungle. This is the account of
land, sea, and air units covering the entire six-month battle.
Stories of ordinary privates and seamen, admirals and
generals who survived to claim the victory that was the
turning point of the Pacific War.

KEEPING AUSTRALIA ON THE LEFT

A Catamaran Odyssey Around Australia
by Mark Stewart Darby   ISBN: 1-55571-508-7
                              232 pages, Paperback: $13.95

A wonderful tale of an Australian man, his American
girlfriend, and a small open catamaran called *Tom
Thumb*. It is a precarious adventure that unfolds among
the desolate seaports and motley characters of the
Australian coastline. Sharks, crocodiles, deadly jellyfish,
storms, wild seas, and limestone cliffs are only part of this
unique two-year journey.

OH, WHAT A LOVELY WAR

by Stanley Swift, transcribed and edited by Evelyn Luscher
ISBN: 1-55571-502-8   96 pages, Paperback: $10.95

This book tells you what history books do not. It is war with a human face. It is the unforgettable memoir of British soldier Gunner Stanley Swift through five years of war. Intensely personal and moving, it documents the innermost thoughts and feelings of a young man as he moves from civilian to battle-hardened warrior under the duress of fire.

THROUGH MY EYES

91st Infantry Division, Italian Campaign, 1942-1945
by Leon Weckstein   ISBN: 1-55571-497-8
208 pages, Paperback: $14.95

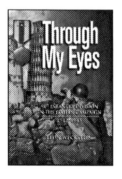

Through My Eyes is the true account of an Average Joe's infantry days before, during, and shortly after the furiously fought battle for Italy. The author's front row seat allows him to report the shocking account of casualties and the rest-time shenanigans during the six weeks of the occupation of the city of Trieste. He also recounts in detail his personal roll in saving the historic Leaning Tower of Pisa.

WORDS OF WAR

From Antiquity to Modern Times   ISBN: 1-55571-491-9
by Gerald Weland   176 pages, Paperback: $13.95

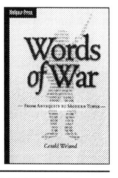

Words of War is a delightful romp through military history. Lively writing leads the reader to an understanding of a number of soldierly quotes. The result of years of haunting dusty libraries, searching obscure journals, and reviewing microfilm files, this unique approach promises to inspire many casual readers to delve further into the circumstances surrounding the birth of many quoted phrases.

TO ORDER OR FOR MORE INFORMATION
1 - 8 0 0 - 2 2 8 - 2 2 7 5 (*telephone*)
info@psi-research.com (*email*)
www.psi-research.com (*Website*)